TWISTED TAILS

SIFTED FACT, FANTASY AND FICTION FROM U.S. COIN HISTORY

BY ROBERT R. VAN RYZIN

Published by

krause publications

700 E. State Street • Iola, WI 54990-0001
Telephone: 715/445-2214

Please call or write for our free catalog of numismatic publications. Our toll-free number to place an order or obtain a free catalog is 800-258-0929 or please use our regular business telephone 715-445-2214 for editorial comment and further information.

Library of Congress Catalog Number: 95-79729
ISBN: 0-87341-393-8

Printed in the United States of America

Table of Contents

Introduction

Why were only five 1913 Liberty Head nickels struck? Who was responsible?

Why are 1804 silver dollars rare despite a recorded mintage of nearly 20,000 coins?

Why are less than 10 examples of the 1894-S dime known. Why were only 24 struck in the first place?

Who were the models for James Earle Fraser's Indian Head nickel? Who modeled for Augustus Saint-Gaudens' attractive $20 gold double eagle? Who designed the Roosevelt dime?

Was the first Standing Liberty quarter considered an indecent coin?

All of these questions, and others like them, have been asked and answered before. Some of these mysteries of U.S. coinage history have been the subject of countless articles, books, and monographs by numismatic writers hoping to shed new light on their background. Yet others have suffered from years of inattention, as collectors assumed there was nothing new to learn or that the stories had already been transcribed correctly by the hobby's scholars and scribes. Some remain, as they were in the beginning, simply "good" stories that enrich the fabric of U.S. coin collecting but likely cannot be proven either way — either because of a lack of documentation or the clouding effects of the passage of time.

Inside you'll find a few of these "twisted tails" covered with jaundiced eye and others simply recounted to establish their place in the folklore and traditions that have grown up around U.S. coinage. In doing so, the attempt here is not to rewrite the history of U.S. coins or to chastise those who may have helped spread ill-based stories, but to raise an awareness that none of the stories surrounding U.S. coins are set in stone, none are sacred, all can and should be re-explored and re-examined — that there is always room for legitimate speculation and question when it comes to numismatic history. Those who stop questioning stop learning.

It is through this questioning that the hobby's knowledge has grown from the time when Charles Barber's halves, quarters and dimes were mistakenly called "Morgans" and collectors held fast to the erroneous belief that the rare 1804 silver dollars were indeed struck in 1804 to today when researchers such as Don Taxay, Eric P. Newman, Walter Breen, Q. David Bowers, R.W. Julian and a legion of others have paved the way to clearing many of the misconceptions that sprang up as the hobby grew and expanding the legitimate history of this nation's coinage.

Presented here, also, are a number of baseless rumors that today may seem humorous to many but in a large way reflect the growth of the nation, the passion Americans feel for their money and the power it holds over them. Some of these are likely quite familiar to collectors, like the rumor that the "JS" initials found on the Roosevelt dime were those of Joseph Stalin. Others are more obscure, having been lost in the pages of the hobby's early publications, where they were first brought forth and readily dismissed for what they were.

The presentation of all, it is hoped, will encourage those who read this to further explore the history of U.S. coins, have some fun questioning what they read, and to search out the hobby's "good" stories for the additional enlightenment and enjoyment it can bring.

— Robert R. Van Ryzin

Chapter 1

What's in a name?

The sordid tale of two Indians by the same name, a nickel, and a bit of acting

Here's a story that's been told and retold to the point where just about every time a collector picks up a magazine or book, it's somehow gone askew.

The story, as it's been told many times before, is that Two Moons, a Cheyenne, and Iron Tail, a Sioux, and a third Indian, whose name sculptor James Earle Fraser couldn't remember, served as models for the Indian Head nickel (1913-1938).

Unfortunately, Fraser's faulty memory along with the coin's life-like depiction of a noble American Indian left the door ajar for several missing "third" models to step through. One of those who eagerly entered and has since taken up permanent residence in the hearts and minds of collectors is Isaac Johnny John, a Seneca of the eastern Iroquois Nation, better known as Chief John Big Tree.

The tale of how he mistakenly came to be accepted as a model for Fraser's work is a fascinating one — wedded to the romance of the Old West, to the desperate plight of the American Indian, to attempts by whites to capitalize on the nation's seemingly unquenchable thirst for fanciful stories of an untamed past, and to artists who sought to capture the Native American's image and spirit on canvas and in magnificent, powerful, and often poignant sculptures.

Against this backdrop, splattered with the paint of a thousand tall

Sculptor James Earle Fraser said his goal in designing the Indian Head nickel (1913-1938) was to create a coin that typified America.

tales, John Big Tree applied his own colorful, if less than truthful, brush, claiming to have been the model for the forehead and the nose of the design. Aided by a great sense of the theatrical, perfected over years of work in Hollywood (including appearances in such early screen epics as John Ford's *The Iron Horse* and *Drums Along the Mohawk*), and early 1960s promotional appearances across the nation, he was able to falsely taint the history of this coin's artistic origins.

Today, through the help of numismatic writers, he has risen to almost a folklore status within the hobby and remains the most mentioned "third" model for Fraser's coin. Forgotten are the glaring inconsistencies in his story that led some writers of his day to dismiss him as a fraud. Overlooked are scattered references to a different "Big Tree," this one a Kiowa, Adoeette, whom evidence suggests is a more likely candidate. Remembered and recounted instead is the old chief's spoon-fed cock-and-bull story that he posed for the nose and forehead of the Indian Head nickel, while a Sioux (Iron Tail) modeled for the cheek and chin of the likeness and a Cheyenne (Two Moons) for the hair and headdress.

Toward a new design

The story of how Chief John Big Tree came to his lofty status begins in 1911, when Fraser responded to Treasury Secretary Franklin MacVeagh's call for a new design to replace the Liberty Head nickel.

With the help of numismatic writers and a bit of acting Chief John Big Tree has risen to an unjustified status within the hobby as the "missing" third model for the Indian Head nickel.

Sculptor James Earle Fraser credited his interest in the American Indian to his upbringing in South Dakota, where he met and made friends with Indians of many of the Great Plains' tribes.

Fraser had already gained international acclaim for his stirring depiction of trail-bitten, downtrodden Indian in his *End of the Trail* statue. He had also endeared himself with President Theodore Roosevelt through sculpting a much-acclaimed bust of the president. The two became fast friends, with Fraser a natural selection as part of Roosevelt's drive to "upgrade" the nation's coinage.

Fraser identified Two Moons, a Cheyenne (left), and Iron Tail, a Sioux, as models for the obverse of the Indian Head nickel. Two Moons was a participant in the famous Battle of the Little Bighorn against Gen. George Armstrong Custer and the U.S. 7th Cavalry. He visited Washington, D.C., on several occasions, including a meeting in 1914 with President Woodrow Wilson. Iron Tail was a famous Oglala Sioux chief who became friends with Buffalo Bill Cody, traveling to Europe in 1889 with Cody's Wild West Show. **Two Moons photograph courtesy of the National Archives. Iron Tail photograph courtesy of The Numismatist.**

The new coin, bearing its realistic representation of an American Indian on the obverse and a bison on the reverse, was released into circulation in 1913. Shortly thereafter the Treasury Department was inundated with letters from the public hoping to learn the identity of the Indian on the new nickel. Unfortunately, Fraser had trouble remembering the names of his models. The question would be broached so many times that many of his responses, each structured in a slightly different manner, appear to reflect his increasing disinterest and distaste for the topic, rather than a true attempt to set the record straight.

An undated (circa 1913) letter to Mint Director George E. Roberts suggests that Fraser considered the Indian design represented a type, rather than a direct portrait. The question of the models was apparently of secondary importance to the artist.

He said he could recall Two Moons, a Cheyenne, and Iron Tail, a Sioux, as having served as the inspiration. Also, possibly, "one or two others." In later years he dropped the number of possible "other" models to one, and at times shrugged off such inquiries, directing his secretary to provide the stock answer. [1]

The initial press coverage on the new coin was also unclear. An article by D.H. De Shon, of the Utica, N.Y., *Herald-Dispatch*, reprinted in the May 1913 issue of *The Numismatist*, erroneously proclaimed the design showed an "artistically executed head of a Comanche Indian."[2] The March issue of *The Numismatist* more correctly reported that it was based on a Cheyenne who visited Fraser in New York.[3]

Kodak snap-shootin'

One Indian not mentioned by Fraser who quickly captured public attention and acceptance as one of the models was Chief Two Guns White Calf, a Blackfoot. Two Guns' claim lost a great deal of validity however when, in 1931, Fraser vigorously denied having used him as a model.

A copy of a June 10, 1931, letter from Fraser to the Commissioner of Indian Affairs of the U.S. Department of the Interior (released to the press on July 12, 1931) quotes Fraser as saying:

> "The Indian head on the Buffalo nickel is not a direct portrait of any particular Indian, but was made from several portrait busts which I did of Indians. As a matter of fact, I used three different heads; I remember two of the men. One was Irontail, the best Indian head I can remember; the other one was Two Moons, and the third I cannot recall.
>
> I have never seen Two Guns Whitecalf nor used him in any way, although he has a magnificent head. I can easily understand how he was mistaken in thinking that he posed for me. A great many artists have modeled and drawn him, and it was only natural for him to believe that one of them was the designer of the nickel. I think he is undoubtedly honestly of the opinion that his portrait is on the nickel.
>
> I am particularly interested in Indian affairs, having as a boy lived in South Dakota before the Indians were so carefully guarded in their agencies. Later, the Crow Creek agency was formed at Chamberlain, but I always feel that

Two Guns White Calf, also known as John Two Guns or John White-
calf Two Guns, was perhaps the most photographed Indian of his
day. It's likely he honestly came to believe that his profile appeared
on Fraser's Indian Head nickel. **Courtesy of Spokane Public Library,**
Spokane, Wash.

I have seen the Indian in his natural habitat, with his finest costumes being worn. I hope their affairs are progressing favorably." [4]

A clue to how Two Guns White Calf became convinced that his likeness was used on the nickel, and how the legend continued to flourish despite Fraser's denial, comes from an article by syndicated columnist Elmo Scott Watson published in various newspapers in 1938, as the Indian Head nickel was being supplanted by the new Jefferson type. [5]

Watson wrote that Two Guns bore such a striking resemblance to the Indian on the nickel that many who visited the chief at Montana's Glacier National Park thought they were viewing the coin's model. So did the Indian, who Watson says, honestly believed that the coin was designed after his likeness.

"So the legend persisted and when the Blackfoot died in 1934, the familiar story (with pictures, of course) blossomed out in full flower again, thus proving that error, as well as truth, when 'crushed to earth will rise again.' "

Watson said it was hard to trace the origin of the story, but provided the following, given to him by Hoke Smith, western development agent of the Great Northern Railroad:

> "You asked for it, I consulted the sages of the tribe, and here is the real story of the Indian face upon the nickel, as near as I can translate it from the Blackfoot spoken and sign language:
>
> Many moons ago, when he was in his early thirties, the late Chief Two Guns White Calf, chief of the Glacier National Park Blackfoot tribe, got his first nickel from one of the earlier spendthrift tourists that came to his tepee, kodak snap-shootin'. It was one of the buffalo series of five-cent pieces.
>
> Two Guns was delighted with the picture of the Buffalo, which side happened to be 'tails up' when the generous tourist put it in the palm of his hand. A moment later, when he turned the coin over and beheld his own likeness standing in bold relief before him, it was as lookin' into a mirror to Two Guns.
>
> 'Me!' he exclaimed. 'Big White Chief put warrior on penny. But when it come to nickel only chief is big enough.' It happened the 'liberal-handed' tourist Two Guns was talking to was a news photographer 'grabbing some photo fea-

ture' stuff while visiting the park. Straightaway he went out and seized the buffalo nickel Indian feature and gave it wide circulation.

While Two Guns White Calf lived (for twenty years after) he was hailed by every school child in the United States as the Indian whose face appeared on the buffalo nickel. And there was much controversy throughout the land!"

Two Guns still has his advocates. In 1989 the question of his posing for the nickel was raised in a feature for the Feb. 27 issue of *Antique Week*. The article, "Two Guns White Calf — A Model Indian?", by associate editor Don Johnson, detailed the beliefs of Charles Bevard of Bevco Auctions, Hampstead, Md., who in March of that year auctioned off portions of the chief's personal affects.

Featured in the auction were many museum-quality items, including clothing, Indian-related advertising items from the 1927 Fair of the Iron Horse, and a curious three-inch diameter medallion that resembled the Indian Head nickel and carried Two Guns' personal mark on the back.

The article detailed how Bevard came upon the artifacts and why he began to explore the background of this famous Native American.

According to Bevard, it was an auction of 30 or 40 stoneware crocks that led him to believe that Two Guns modeled for the nickel. In a somewhat backhanded way, the auction resulted in the unexpected discovery of Indian clothing, headdresses, medicine bags, a horse effigy pipe and the Indian Head nickel medallion — all of which was stored in three suitcases in the basement of the pharmacy of Frank McGinity, a third-generation pharmacist in the Highlandtown area of east Baltimore.

The discovery of the medal, and the background story McGinity related, led Bevard to search newspaper and archival holdings in an attempt to prove that Two Guns was the model for the Indian Head nickel, and, more importantly, to raise awareness of the lost heritage of the American Indian.

Bevard's research showed that Two Guns was born in 1871 and was adopted at an early age. Two Guns' father, White Calf, was a prominent warrior chief and responsible for many of the tribe's treaties. When White Calf died, in 1903, Two Guns became one of the tribal leaders.

Bevard believed one of two things happened: Either Two Guns came to honestly believe he was the model for the Indian Head nick-

Two Guns' nickel medallion, presented to him sometime prior to his September 1927 meeting with President Calvin Coolidge. **Courtesy of Charles Bevard.**

el (this through the efforts of railroad magnate and promoter James J. Hill) or Two Guns actually served as the model but the government forced Fraser to deny Two Guns' association with the coin.

According to Bevard, sometime around 1912, Hill, who was at one point undisputed master of one-third of the railroad facilities in the West, began looking for a means to promote tourism to Montana's "land of shining mountains," Glacier National Park. At that time, Hill's Great Northern Railroad owned the more than 1-million-acre park adjacent to the Blackfoot Indian Reservation, and between 1910 and 1917 spent $1.5 million readying the park to receive tourists.

To promote travel to the West and, perhaps, to advance the belief that the once Wild West had now been tamed for tourism, Hill came up with the idea of using the Blackfeet Indians, who formerly laid claim to the land, on country-hopping tours by rail.

Hill's Great Northern Railroad would transport tribe members and their chief to various central and eastern U.S. cities. Bevard says photographs still exist showing Two Guns and members of his tribe perched on Chicago rooftops.

During their travels, the Indians also patiently posed for various artists and were the subject of one of the railroad's promotional calendars.

A 1927 trip brought Two Guns and his tribe to Maryland and the Fair of the Iron Horse, the centennial celebration of the Baltimore and Ohio Railroad.

On Sept. 17, 1927, one week prior to the fair's opening, Two Guns and the tribe met with President Calvin Coolidge at the White House. Two Guns appeared in a group photograph sporting a newly received medallion resembling the Indian Head nickel. When he arrived at the fair, the B & O brochure proclaimed that he had indeed served as a model for the coin.

Bevard came to the conclusion that the "official or unofficial" presentation of the medallion, along with the size and scope of the fair, which drew 1.3 million people over its three-week run, combined to convince the chief that he was portrayed on the nickel. Bevard speculated that this may have been Hill's intention, to transform Two Guns into a complete promotional package.

It would have been easy to do. After all, the official brochure for the fair informed visitors that Two Guns was the model; a medallion presented to the chief prior to his meeting with the Great White Chief likely reinforced the story in his mind; Two Guns bore an undeniable resemblance to the nickel; and Two Guns had modeled for many artists, Fraser may have been one of them.

"They took this Indian somewhere in Washington [D.C.] and led him to believe that he was being officially blessed with a portrait of himself on a medallion of the Buffalo nickel," Bevard said. "He wore that around his neck for the rest of his life. When he came back from Washington he was a complete package for the rest of the fair." [6]

Two Guns shown in a portion of a group photograph taken during his visit to the White House in 1927. Two Guns is wearing the medallion given to him prior to his attendance at the Fair of the Iron Horse where he was touted as the model for the Indian Head nickel. Courtesy of Charles Bevard.

Bevard's other theory involved the testimony of Mary Ground, then the oldest living member of the Blackfoot tribe.

Ground, who at one time performed ceremonial dances with Two Guns at Glacier National Park, told Bevard of a meeting, sometime around 1910 or 1911, with President William Howard Taft, probably held at the park's Many Glaciers Hotel.

It was at this meeting, according to Ground, that Taft announced that Two Guns was to serve as a model for the nickel.

Bevard admitted he could not find record of the meeting, despite Ground's testimony that it was covered by as many as 50 reporters arriving on horseback, but, he added, Taft traveled into Montana several times during 1909.

"So her story may actually be true," he said. "But, anyway, I don't see the reason for her to lie, as she had no idea to expect me or anything like that." [7]

Bevard suggested that the government may have wanted to "knock the wind out of Two Guns" by having Fraser deny that the tribal leader was a model for the Indian Head nickel. This because Two Guns, who headed a secret organization known as the Mad Dog Society, was attempting to preserve Blackfoot heritage. Traditional Indian dances such as the Sun Dance and the Ghost Dance, which had been forbidden by the government, were again being performed after American Indians received blanket citizenship in 1924.

Bevard said someone may have feared that Two Guns would again take the fierce Blackfeet warriors on the warpath in an attempt to regain their land — something the government did not want to happen.

"If he wasn't a model for the Buffalo nickel, he was the most famous Indian chief in the 20th century," Bevard said. "And he was the transition that is probably needed today in bridging the gap, to create a healing process. He did have a relationship with non-Indians, anyone from the president on down, and he did a lot of great things for Indians and he was quite the statesman, and, if nothing else, he should be remembered for that. But it's a shame that we can't find some documentation." [8]

Murky waters

One of the first numismatic writers to wade into the murky waters surrounding the design controversy was Marianne F. Miller. Her article, "Buffaloed by the Buffalo Nickel," in the October 1956 issue of *Numismatic Scrapbook Magazine*, lent wishful support to Two Guns

White Calf as the missing model while at the same time offhandedly dismissed Chief John Big Tree as a possible candidate.

Miller said her search for the identity of the third Indian was sparked by an item appearing in the September 1955 issue of *Numismatic Scrapbook Magazine*, which told of the arrest of Chief John Big Tree, 79, in Syracuse, N.Y., for driving while intoxicated. The notice said the Indian claimed to be one of the models for the Indian Head nickel.

Miller set out to contact John Big Tree, but found him "not in the least cooperative." She added that she found "no other evidence to substantiate his claim." [9]

Miller said that after visiting the Treasury Department, the Bureau of Indian Affairs, and the National Archives over an 11-month period, along with writing 39 letters in an attempt to determine the name of the third model, she was sure of only one thing, "the buffalo nickel really had me buffaloed."

As part of her presentation, Miller argued that the U.S. Mint would not have allowed Fraser to directly portray any living person on the coin, implying that his statement about using a composite portrait may have been purposely aimed at disguising Two Guns' role in the design. It would also justify the artist's denial of ever using Two Guns as a model.

Her article is largely devoted to quotes from people who knew Two Guns, most of whom believed he was the model. Forrest R. Stone, superintendent of the Flathead Indian Agency in Dixon, Mont., who was with Two Guns when he died, told Miller he believed Two Guns' story; Frank Sherburne, who had lived on the Blackfoot reservation since 1896 and was well acquainted with Two Guns, expressed his belief that Two Guns was the model; and Waldon S. Arnholt, an artist from Ashland, Ohio, who had used Two Guns as a model, was positive that the portrait on the nickel was of Two Guns, right down to the eyes, ears, nose and mouth.

But when Frank Sherburne questioned Two Guns as to whether or not he was the model, Miller says, the chief admitted he did not know.

A lot of people had painted him, Two Guns apparently confided to Sherburne, but Two Guns said he kept his braids better than those on the coin, and when he wore a feather "it pointed up from the back of his head and not down like a whipped bird!" [10]

On request, Two Guns would also sign Indian Head nickels (for a premium) with his mark — two crossed rifles for the coins and two rifles and a young calf on pictures. He would even furnish the nickel. [11]

Enter stage right

Irked by Miller's story, Leonard J. Ratzman entered the fray in "The Buffalo Nickel, A 50-Year-Old Mystery," appearing in two parts in the May and June 1964 issues of the *Whitman Coin Journal*. Ratzman wrote:

> "In every source of reference researched by this writer and others attempting to solve the same problem, it is agreed that the Cheyenne Two Moons and the Sioux Chief Iron Tail are definitely two of the three Indians used as models by Fraser. The identity of the third, however, has still not been identified after half a century and has eluded every effort to be found." [12]

Citing Fraser's denial, Ratzman came to the conclusion that Two Guns White Calf was not the model. Ratzman based his conclusion primarily on a July 1931 issue of the American Numismatic Association's journal, *The Numismatist*, which reprinted a widely circulated Associated Press dispatch, noting:

> "That is not the face of Chief Two Guns Whitecalf on the Buffalo nickel. It is three other fellows, says an Associated Press dispatch.
>
> Ever since the present 5-cent piece was designed, about eighteen years ago, there have been stories to the effect that Two Guns was the original of the Indian head. Recently James E. Frazer [sic], who designed the coin, wrote the Indian Office that he had never seen Two Guns, but had used three different Indians to obtain the design. One was named Irontail, another Two Moons, a Cheyenne chief who is now dead. Frazer [sic] has forgotten the name of the other. Nevertheless Chief Two Guns has a magnificent head and many artists have modeled it." [13]

To prove that Chief John Big Tree deserved the honor, Ratzman said a meeting he had with the Indian in September 1962 was the "first in a long line of events that have led to what is felt to be the solving of the identity of the third Indian." [14]

At the time, John Big Tree was being billed as one of the main attractions of the Eastern States Exposition in Springfield, Mass. According to Ratzman, advance publicity for the event named John Big Tree, 97, as a model for the Indian Head nickel and provided biographical information.

Ratzman said John Big Tree was born near the end of the Civil War, "the son of helmsman aboard a Great Lakes steamer." By the time he was 14, John Big Tree had been bitten by the acting bug. He began to travel, moving from town to town by Indian wagon caravan, performing in nightly stands. The chief would later spend 35 years in Hollywood as an actor.

Given his chance to meet with John Big Tree, something Miller had found impossible, Ratzman inexplicably opted not to ask the chief if he had posed for the nickel.

"After meeting the Chief, this writer did not want to run into the same brick wall that Miss Miller did, so no attempt was made at the time to verify his claim," Ratzman wrote.[15] It was only after months of correspondence with the chief's publicity agent that Ratzman said a breakthrough came. The agent suggested he contact Dr. E. A. Bates, "an expert in Indian lore" who at one time worked in the Agriculture Department of Cornell University.

Bates' reply to Ratzman, dated June 24, 1963, tells of a meeting Bates claimed he had with Le Roy Fess, a feature writer for the *Buffalo News*. Though no date is given for the meeting, if it occurred, it must have taken place sometime prior to the release of the nickel.

Bates told Ratzman that he had been in New York to give a speech when he met Fess. Fess, in turn, told Bates that he saw Fraser "pick up Big Tree while the Indian was modeling for class in the Buffalo Art Museum." Bates wrote:

> "That night, I saw John [Big Tree] on the Tonawanda (Seneca) reservation and I said, 'Well, John, I hear (from Fess) you are going to be on a coin.' He said no, but the drawer (artist) only wanted his nose. John's wife, Cynthia, said I should cut off some of John's nose, he's always in other people's business. One time at the Indian Village, a little while later, a man gave John a dollar for a photo and John said, 'That's more than I got for the Nickel.' " [16]

Ratzman believed his search was over. For that matter, so did many numismatists.

Aided by Ratzman's bold article — published only a few months prior to a *Coin World* reprint of an article that identified the Kiowa Adoeette (Big Tree) as the third model — Chief John Big Tree was catapulted to the forefront. [17]

Don Taxay, in his 1966 book, *The U.S. Mint and Coinage: An Illustrated History From 1776 to the Present*, was caught up in the belief that Chief John Big Tree was the third model and refers to Ratzman's article as the source. Other writers since have variously named "Chief John Tree," "Big Tree," "Chief John Big Tree" or, sometimes, "John Big Tree, Kiowa," but generally intending reference to the Seneca/Iroquois Indian, not the Kiowa, Adoeette.

The belief that John Big Tree worked as a model for Fraser was amplified by the Indian's own efforts and the public's willingness to embrace him as a living symbol of America. The old Indian was regularly depicted in a nostalgic, Old West fashion — next to a tepee, standing with a bison or in full headdress.

When he visited Wisconsin in 1964 to help celebrate the city of Waupun's 125th anniversary, he graciously posed with a symbolic outstretched arm before a rare bronze original of Fraser's *End of the Trail* statue, located in the city's cemetery.

Chief John Big Tree toured the country in the 1960s claiming to have modeled for the forehead and nose of the Indian Head nickel's design. He also made an appearance on the popular television show **What's My Line** *where he pitched himself as one of three models for the coin.*

22

Fraser's famous End of the Trail *statue, located in the cemetery at Waupun, Wis. The first* End of the Trail *statue to be bronzed, it was presented to the city in the 1920s by industrialist Clarence A. Shaler. The first modeling of an* End of the Trail *statue dates to the late 1800s, when Fraser created a smaller version, winning a prize in an 1898 art competition. A full-scale plaster* End of the Trail *was displayed at the Panama-Pacific Exposition in San Francisco in 1915. It became the topic of a series unauthorized reproductions, including a painting by another artist transformed into prints and distributed nationally. Photo by the author.*

23

During that same period he made a guest appearance on the popular television show *What's My Line*, where he successfully stumped a panel of celebrities. His line was that he posed for the nose and forehead of the famous coin.

For the cover photo of the March 1964 issue of *Esquire*, John Big Tree showed up at the magazine's studio wearing a business suit, overcoat and sporting a crew cut.

He told author Alice Glaser that he posed for the nickel in 1917 and received his first nickel the following year.[18] Glaser corrected his dates, stating that Fraser had seen the chief working a Wild West show on Coney Island in the summer of 1912 and had asked him to pose for the nickel. John Big Tree, she said, resisted, wanting to wait until the show season was over.

A plaster for the Indian Head nickel, dated 1912.

He began posing, she said, in November of that year and continued working for the artist through April of the following year — arriving at the artist's studio in the morning to model for the nickel and in the afternoon for the painting [sic, sculpture?] *End of the Trail.*

Unfortunately for the would-be model, first examples of the new coin entered circulation in February 1913, a month prior to the end of his supposed six-month stint as a model and long after initial plaster models had been prepared. Also, it's doubtful that a skilled artist would have needed six months of the Indian's time to capture the look of his forehead and nose.

John Big Tree, it should be remembered, was an actor. He regularly played roles as Great Plains Indians in Hollywood. His appearance at *Esquire* was likely no different, just another acting job.

The record of John Big Tree's visit to the magazine's studio lends considerable insight into how a bit of makeup, an appropriate wig, and proper feathers could help convince the public that the illusion before them was real.

Make-over miracles

Glaser had written that when 87-year-old Isaac Johnny John entered Carl Fischer's studio for the photograph that would eventually grace the magazine's cover, the Indian was wearing a business suit and overcoat, with his hair in a crew cut. With a bit of help, an hour later he emerged from a dressing room dutifully made up in a black wig, makeup and wearing buckskin trousers.

A makeup artist then applied color to the chief's skin, explaining that "People expect red Indians to look red," and stuffed cotton wadding in the chief's mouth to fill the void where teeth used to be. This done, the illusion was completed. With an Indian Head nickel as a model, black and white feathers were positioned in the Indian's wig. A cut-up red bandana wrapped his newly made braids.[19]

Chief John Big Tree was thereby made to resemble the nickel — so much so that upon seeing a copy of the magazine cover the artist's wife Laura Gardin Fraser is said to have identified him as a model for her husband's coin.

Writers Annette R. Cohen and Ray M. Druley, in *The Buffalo Nickel*, quote an April 17, 1964, letter from Laura Gardin Fraser to the Mint director. In it, she says, "the name of Big Tree always came to my mind" in relation to the third model for the Indian Head nickel, but that she wasn't certain until she saw the *Esquire* cover, sent to her on the occasion of the chief's 100th birthday.[20]

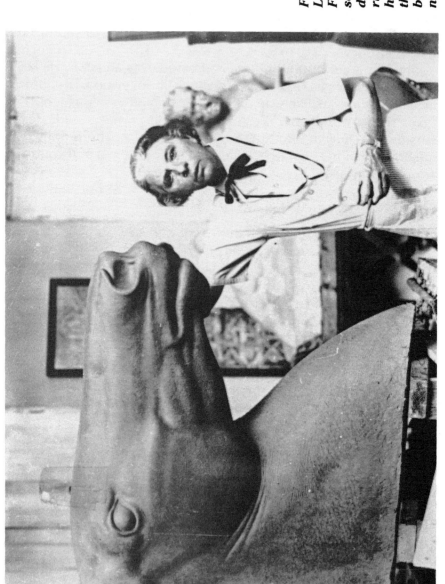

Fraser's wife, Laura Gardin Fraser, a noted sculptor and coin designer in her own right, claimed to have remembered the third model as being an Indian named Big Tree.

Mrs. Fraser added that it was amazing that the chief had changed so little over the years. Surprisingly, she said she had never seen Iron Tail or Two Moons, this because she wasn't at the studio much during the time the coin was being modeled. The Frasers weren't married until 1913, after the nickel was released.

Frankly, at 100, or even 87 as the *Esquire* article notes, it's just not possible that John Big Tree hadn't changed much in appearance since 1911, when the first plaster models are believed to have been made. The cover photo depicts an aged Indian, something John Big Tree was not in 1911.

Of significance also is that Mrs. Fraser admitted only that she remembered an Indian named Big Tree. Seven years earlier she told a similar story of an Indian named Big Tree, identified by the author of that article as a Kiowa, Adoeette, whose anglicized name was Big Tree.[21]

Noting that "the controversy made for a crowded warpath," Norman Davis in his 1971 book, *The Complete Book of United States Coin Collecting*, wrote that "Chief John Big Tree (Seneca) believed for over 50 years that the coin showed him; when he died, newspapers honored his claim — until they began hearing from collectors who pointed out that he had no proof of the claim."[22]

If there was an outcry from collectors, as Davis suggests, it doesn't seem to have carried much weight in the long run, as today it has largely disappeared from the numismatic landscape.

One numismatic writer who long ago questioned Chief John Big Tree's inability to remember his age was Lee Martin. In his 1966 book, *Coin Columns*, Martin said that after being arrested for drunken driving in 1955 Chief John Big Tree gave his age as 79; seven years later he was claiming to be 92; two years after that he was 97. In 1966, one year before his death, he was 102. (At a Texas Numismatic Association convention that same year he told *Numismatic News* he was 104.)

"Evidently arithmetic was not his forte," Martin wrote, adding that if Chief John Big Tree was 79 in 1955 he would have been about 36 in 1912 when the coin was being modeled. Iron Tail and Two Moons were much older. Martin argued that it seemed questionable "that a skilled sculptor would have used one subject so different from the other portions in a composition. If, however, he truly is 101 years old today, then the story becomes more likely."[23]

Years later, writer Clement Bailey took a similar tack, observing that John Big Tree had learned his story well but had adopted "new math" before it was invented.

Chief John Big Tree claimed he posed for the "painting" End of the Trail in 1917. There was a painting, but it wasn't by Fraser. A veteran of the silent film era, John Big Tree regularly posed in Old West fashion, playing up his claim as the model for the nickel and the statue. These photographs were taken in Waupun, Wis., on the occasion of the city's 125th anniversary.

28

Chief John Big Tree at the Texas Numismatic Association convention in 1966 where he distributed wooden nickels promoting Falstaff Breweries.

PRESENTED BY
CHIEF
JOHN BIG TREE
ORIGINAL HEAD ON
THE BUFFALO NICKEL
GALVESTON, TEXAS
MARCH 26, 1966

Unfortunately for John Big Tree, after his death on July 6, 1967, records kept by the Onondaga Historical Association showed him to be only 92 years old, meaning he was 36 in 1911 when the plasters of the Indian Head nickel were completed. By contrast, Iron Tail was 61 and Two Moons was 64. Adoeette was 64.

Adoeette, "Big Tree." **Courtesy National Archives.**

An Associated Press obituary notice, datelined on the day of his death, told that the chief's Christian name was Isaac Johnny John and that he had played more than 100 minor parts in early Western movies, often describing himself as the "best bareback rider in Hollywood." Further, Isaac Johnny John claimed to have been born in 1862 "and sometimes showed an Indian head penny of that year, which he said was given to him by his grandfather as proof" of his age.

Reporting on Chief John Big Tree's attendance at the 1966 Texas Numismatic Association convention in Galveston, where the chief signed and gave away wooden nickels as part of a promotion for Falstaff Breweries, the April 25, 1966, issue of *Numismatic News* said:

> "Chief John Big Tree, who claims to be 104 years old, is a full blooded Iroquois who now lives with his wife on the Onondaga Reservation near Syracuse, New York. He was one of three Indians selected to pose for the design of the buffalo nickel in 1912. The coin shows a buffalo on the reverse and an Indian on the obverse.
>
> According to the Chief, he was used as the model for the nose and forehead of the Indian nickel while a Sioux modeled for the cheek and chin of the likeness and a Cheyenne for the hair and headdress.
>
> The idea of the portrait on the nickel was to represent the typical American Indian which resulted in three different tribes being used as models.

Chief Big Tree says he was working in a Coney Island show when he was chosen to pose, 'because of his classic facial features.'

He says he also posed for the famous art work, 'The End Of The Trail' at the same time he was posing for the U.S. coin. He posed for the picture in the mornings and the coin in the afternoons.

Questions have been raised regarding the Indian's age, but Chief John Big Tree says he has an Indian head cent dated 1862 which his grandfather gave him at the end of the Civil War and told him 'never to part with the coin as it was struck in the year of Chief Big Tree's birth.'

The Chief claims to still have the cent, which in his opinion, is proof of the year in which he was born." [24]

Simple logic also brings John Big Tree's claim into doubt. Fraser grew up in South Dakota, where, he said, he counted Indians of several tribes, including the Dakotas, Sioux and Kiowa, as his friends. Several writers have recorded that his files were filled with photographs of Great Plains Indians. It's not likely that he needed to, or would have, relied on the features of an Indian from an eastern tribe when there were so many plains Indians from which to choose. Although the design may have been a composite, it was, in Fraser's own words, intended to reflect the Indians of the Great Plains.

New York bound

The truth as to who, if anyone, was the missing third model most likely lies in a quote found in Dean Krakel's 1973 book *End of the Trail: Odyssey of a Statue.*

Through Fraser's unpublished memoirs, interviews with Laura Gardin Fraser and a host of other sources, Krakel thoroughly documented the careers of James Earle Fraser and Laura Gardin Fraser, while detailing his own efforts as director of the National Cowboy Hall of Fame to transfer and restore one of the remaining full-size *End of the Trail* statues.

In reference to the coin, he quotes Fraser as saying:

"In designing it, my objective was to achieve a coin which would be truly America, that could not be confused with currency of any other country. I made sure, therefore, to use none of the attributes which other nations had in the past. And in my search for symbols, I found no motif

Kiowas Adoeette (left) and White Bear, who led an 1871 raid on an Army supply train heading for Fort Richardson, Texas. Both were convicted of first-degree murder and sentenced to hang. Their death sentence gained considerable attention from humanitarians in the East, leading to their conditional release in 1873. Adoeette later converted to Christianity, serving as a deacon at the Rainy Mountain Indian Mission for 30 years. **Courtesy Texas State Archives.**

within the boundaries of the United States so distinctive as the American buffalo, or bison. The great herds of buffalo that roamed the Western plains played an important epic in winning the West.

With the Indian head on the obverse, we have perfect unity in theme. It has pertinent historical significance, and is in line with the best traditions of coin design, where the purpose was to memorialize a nation or a people."[25]

Krakel adds that the Treasury Department received hundreds of letters asking the identity of the Indian model for the coin. Fraser, he said, wrote:

"In fact, the profile is a composite of three plains Indians — a Sioux, a Kiowa, and a Cheyenne. The three Indians were Iron Tail, a Sioux; Big Tree, a Kiowa; and Two Moons, a Cheyenne. The Indians had come to visit President Roosevelt and stopped off in New York. During this time, I was able to study and photograph them. The three had combined features of the hardy, virile types of Great Plains Indian."[26]

Unfortunately, Krakel misattributed this quote, the proceeding one, and one concerning the bison, Black Diamond, to Watson's article from the *Oceana Herald*. The correct attribution has not been located.[27]

The same quotes appear in William Bridges' 1974 work *Gathering of Animals: An Unconventional History of the New York Zoological Society* but without reference to source.

The misattributed bison quote, which by tone appears to be from the same source as Fraser's comments about the Indians, has been reproduced elsewhere and matches similar statements by Fraser. [28]

Any such visit by these Indians to New York would likely have occurred between 1901 and 1909, while Roosevelt was still in office. We know from Fraser's background that he was well acquainted with Roosevelt, having been recommended by Augustus Saint-Gaudens (for whom he was then serving as a studio assistant) to take on one of Saint-Gaudens' commissions — a bust of the president from life.

Fraser and Roosevelt shared a common interest in the West. It's not unlikely, therefore, that Roosevelt, aware of Fraser's interest in studying Indians, sent Two Moons, Big Tree and Iron Tail to see him.

A suggestive reference by editor Edgar Adams in the March 1913 issue of *The Numismatist*, seems to lend some credence, though no positive proof. Adams related:

> "It is said the Mr. Fraser (the designer) took as a model an Indian of the Cheyenne tribe, who recently visited New York City." [29]

Two Moons is known to have traveled to Washington, D.C., and New York on a number of occasions. In fact, in February 1913, just after the nickel's release, the *New York Times* listed him among 30 or more chiefs visiting New York, including Sioux and Kiowa, for the dedication of a monument to the American Indian. Iron Tail, who traveled in a number of the famous Wild West shows, was also a frequent visitor to the East.

The positive identification of the Kiowa Adoeette as the model would certainly help to explain the confusion that has plagued numismatic writers since the early 1970s and 1980s. It's not at all unusual to find a writer name John Big Tree as the model, only to then show a National Archives' photograph of Adoeette; or identify John Big Tree as a Kiowa, not a Seneca.

An act of war

Is it possible that Adoeette modeled? It certainly isn't without reason. Adoeette was a well-known Kiowa chief and likely made visits to the East, as many in his tribe did.

He was also much more famous in his day than John Big Tree — his fame coming not from movie roles but from his real-life actions.

In 1871, Adoeette, along with Kiowa Chief White Bear, was convicted of first-degree murder and sentenced to die by hanging for his part in a gruesome raid on an Army supply train heading for Fort Richardson, Texas. Seven men were killed. The Indians, under White Bear's leadership, mutilated the living and the dead.

One teamster was found chained to his wagon, his tongue cut out; the teamster was burned to death.

Following their arrest and conviction, the fates of Adoeette and White Bear became the focus of humanitarian groups in the East, hoping to stay their execution. Even the Indian Bureau claimed that they had committed an act of war, not murder.

The judge presiding at their trial wrote to Texas Gov. Edmund Davis suggesting a change in the sentence to life imprisonment at hard labor.

Public pressure finally led to their conditional release in 1873.

The Indians were warned not to leave the reservation or they would go back to prison.

They did leave, however, and were again arrested in 1874. Adoeette and White Bear were taken to Fort Sill, Okla., where Adoeette was imprisoned and held until the following year. White Bear was sent back to Texas to serve a life sentence.

Adoeette later converted to Christianity and spent 30 years as a deacon for the Rainy Mountain Indian Mission. He died at Fort Sill on Nov. 13, 1929.

One biographer said, "he became a model of peaceful serenity in his old age." It is also most likely he became a model for a famous U.S. coin now incorrectly attributed to an Indian with the same name.

Chapter 2

A model bison

The flip side of the Indian Head nickel saga

All right. So there is serious disagreement as to which Indians modeled for the obverse of James Earle Fraser's Indian Head nickel, but what about the bison on the reverse — Is it Black Diamond? Well . . .

Despite the best intentions of numismatists to get this story straight, it's just about as twisted as any in the fable-strewn numismatic stable.

Fine specimen?

First, who was Black Diamond? By some accounts he was the finest specimen of a bison in captivity. By others, he was mangy, droopy-headed, suicide-prone animal who made a timely trip to the dinner table as a high-priced steak.

Depending on which account you read, he was housed either at the Central Park Corral, Garden City Zoological Gardens, the Bronx Zoological Park, the New York Central Zoo, the Central Park Corral or the Bronx Park Zoo.

Unfortunately, as with the story of the models for the Indian on the obverse, the artist hasn't been much help. Fraser said of the animal:

"He was not a plains buffalo, but none other than Black Diamond, the contrariest animal in the Bronx Park Zoo. I stood for hours watching and catching his form and mood in plastic clay. Black Diamond was less conscious of the honor being conferred on him than of the annoyance which he suffered from insistent gazing upon him. He refused point blank to permit me to get side views of him, and stubbornly showed his front face most of the time." [1]

Fraser's reference to a Bronx Park Zoo would cause confusion for some time to come. Add to that the Jan. 27, 1913, issue of the *New York Herald* which made a similar observation, noting that the animal was a typical specimen found grazing in the New York Zoological Park (more commonly known as the Bronx Zoo). [2]

Under the traditional story, however, Black Diamond was born in the Central Park Zoo, not the Bronx Zoo, in 1893 from Barnum & Bailey stock and lived until 1915. Or, in a slightly different version, he was a Barnum & Bailey circus buffalo, *retired* to the Central Park Zoo.

The December 1915 issue of *The Numismatist* also placed Black Diamond at Central Park. Reporting on the bison's death, the journal said:

This photograph, supposedly of Black Diamond, has appeared in print on a number of occasions, including a prior issue of Coins *magazine.*

Original drawings by James Earle Fraser for the reverse of the Indian Head nickel. Courtesy of the Cowboy Hall of Fame and Western History Center.

"Black Diamond, the aged buffalo, whose likeness is printed on our $10 legal tender notes and is stamped on the last issue of five-cent pieces, was put to death in New York on November 17. He was about 20 years old and the largest bison in captivity. He had been an inmate of the Central Park corral for many years. Black Diamond's hide, which measured 13 by 13 feet, will be made into an automobile robe. The bison weighed 1,550 pounds, from which 750 pounds dressed meat was obtained. The teeth were in a remarkable state of preservation. The head, which will be mounted, sold for a considerable amount of money. The bison was killed because of old age. He was sold in the surplus live-stock auction last summer and was left at the park subject to the call of his purchaser." [3]

The price, by some accounts, was $700, with the carcass sold to A. Silz Poultry and Game. Silz had the head mounted and sold the meat as "Black Diamond Steaks" at good prices.

The head later came into the possession of Benjamin H. Mayer, an employee of Hoffman & Mayer Inc., the firm that took over from Silz. It remained on display at the firm until Hoffman & Mayer closed its doors in 1978. In 1985, the head was shown at the American Numismatic Association convention in Baltimore.

It may just be a case of a mixed-up identification by the artist and the *Herald* between the Bronx Zoo, a full-scale zoo, and the Central Park Menagerie (or corral), a small, penned-in display of animals, but even into the 1970s, when William Bridges (then curator of publications at the New York Zoological Society) wrote *Gathering of Animals: An Unconventional History of the New York Zoological Society*, the Bronx Zoo was still receiving queries as to Black Diamond, but could find no record of the zoo ever owning an animal by that name!

A sad failure

The confusion, Bridges said, could be traced as far back as William T. Hornaday, first director of the New York Zoological Park. Hornaday was responsible for bringing a herd of bison to the park to graze on a special 20-acre range. [4]

In November 1915 one correspondent wrote to Hornaday:

"I see in the paper a notice of the death of the big bison 'Black Diamond,' or 'Toby' as he was familiarly known. It has been stated that Black Diamond was the model for the buffalo on the ten dollar bill, also the five-cent nickle [*sic.*]

If that is so it does not do him justice and was enough to make him ill. Was Black Diamond in the Central Park collection of animals or was he in the Zoological Park? The paper stated he was confined in Central Park." [5]

Bridges could find no record of Hornaday's response. But to a similar inquiry, wanting to know how the animal came by its name, Hornaday replied that the buffalo named Black Diamond was a Central Park animal, which the Bronx Zoo had nothing to do with. Hornaday added that it was possible that the name had been bestowed on an animal by Billy Snyder, Central Park's head keeper. [6]

Yet, he wondered, "if 'Black Diamond' was as fine an animal as we are asked to believe, then I cannot understand why he should be sold to a butcher at a cut price."

Hornaday was certain, however, that Black Diamond was not the animal that served as the model for the $10 bill. Hornaday said he visited the Smithsonian Institution when the glass front of an exhibit of bison (which he mounted in the 1880s while chief taxidermist at the Smithsonian) was removed so that photographs could be taken in preparation of the new $10 bill. [7]

Bridges also quotes a Jan. 7, 1918, letter from Martin S. Garretson, secretary of the Bison Society, to Hornaday in which the secretary was looking for a good picture of Black Diamond, the animal formerly in the Central Park Menagerie and believed to have been used on the Indian Head nickel.

Poor wearing qualities led to a change in the reverse design of the Indian Head nickel during its first year of coinage. First strikings (left) showed the bison on raised ground bearing the denomination, "Five Cents." The denomination wore off quickly. The design was therefore altered to recess the wording.

William T. Hornaday, first director of the Bronx Zoo, termed the bison on the nickel a sad failure with its head drooped "as if it had lost all hope in the world." Hornaday said the zoo, referred to by Fraser as the home of the bison model, Black Diamond, never held an animal by that name.

Hornaday replied that the zoo had no information on the animal, but "judging from the character of the buffalo on the nickel, I should say from its dejected appearance" that the animal was likely an inmate of a small menagerie, having lived all of its life in a small enclosure.

"Its head droops as if it had lost all hope in the world, and even the sculptor was not able to raise it," Hornaday wrote. "I regard the bison on the nickel as a sad failure, considered as a work of art." [8]

Garretson, however, attributed the drooping head and tail to the sculptor's need to compress the animal in the coin design. Similarly,

Edgar Adams, editor of *The Numismatist*, who placed Black Diamond as a specimen of the New York Zoological Garden, said:

> "We have no doubt that the original enlarged model of this design was of a handsome character, but that it would not allow for the great reduction to the size of a five-cent piece is quite apparent." [9]

Bridges said additional confusion as to the possible location of a bison named Black Diamond is found in the aforementioned *New York Tribune* article, where the reporter observed that the animal was "grazing." Grazing, he said, would have been possible on the New York Zoological Park's 20 acres, but not at the Central Park Menagerie, which displayed its animals penned in, with no access to grass.

Bridges' theory is that Fraser may have inspected Black Diamond at the Central Park Menagerie, and, after finding him unsuitable, found a better animal at the Bronx Zoo — the dramatic name Black Diamond sticking in his mind when he talked of the model for the coin. [10]

A Bronx tale

Alas, the story should end there. But, as a side note, slightly more than a decade after the announcement of Black Diamond's death, collectors were told that a different animal, ironically named Bronx, served as the model.

The August 1926 issue of *The Numismatist* strangely reported:

> "Bronx, the buffalo whose portrait adorns the buffalo nickel, is no longer king of the Bronx Zoological Park herd, says a press dispatch. His thirty-five year reign ended recently when Cheyenne, a younger bull, challenged his leadership and, after a terrific battle, gored his right side and knocked off one of his horns. After the keepers separated the animals the deposed monarch was exiled to a separate pen and Cheyenne was left to lead the herd." [11]

Chapter 3

An uncertain past

The 1913 Liberty Head nickel's questionable origin and million-dollar future

It's probably every collector's dream to own a truly rare coin — a coin that only a few, if any, others can possess, one rich in history and appeal. It is that spirit, that drive to obtain the obtainable, that has led to the fascinating story of the famed 1913 Liberty Head nickel, a coin that has passed through the hands of the lowly to the collection of a king to become a million-dollar coin.

Worthy plot

The story of the origin and rise in popularity of the 1913 Liberty Head nickel is laced with so much mystery, loosely-based tales of chicanery, and endearing, colorful characters that a Hollywood scriptwriter would be hard-pressed to find a more interesting plot. Among the cast of characters are Col. Edward Howland Robinson Green, son of miserly Hetty Green, the "Witch of Wall Street;" King Farouk, overweight, overbearing playboy ruler of Egypt; Texas coin dealer B. Max Mehl, famous within coin circles for his self-benefiting 1913 Liberty Head nickel reward; and J.V. McDermott, a Milwaukee coin dealer who loved a good drink about as much as he loved his famous "MacNickel."

The story behind the 1913 Liberty Head nickel is one laced in mystery. To date, no one knows for certain why or when the coins were produced, though Samuel Brown, a former Mint employee, is most often charged with the unauthorized minting.

There are other characters as well, all gathered within the folds of a story that began in 1912 and continues to this day. For those schooled in the ways of numismatics, it's an old story. It's the tale of how five examples of a design that was officially retired after 1912 — the Liberty Head by Charles Barber — came to be clandestinely struck at the U.S. Mint in Philadelphia. The culprit, according to legend, was Samuel W. Brown who, it is said, was involved in striking and bringing the illegitimate coins to the 1920 American Numismatic Association convention in Chicago, apparently to stir interest in a future sale.

His marketing campaign successful, Brown disappeared from the numismatic scene, presumably having found a purchaser. The coins next surfaced in 1924 in the possession of Philadelphia dealer August Wagner, later going (apparently as a group) to Col. Green. After Green's death, the coins were dispersed to a number of buyers. Today the whereabouts of only four specimens is known, one having sold in 1993 for just shy of $1 million.

Unknown origins

Certainties are anything but the case in the story behind the creation of the 1913 Liberty Head nickel. What can be said reliably is very limited.

The exact date of the striking of these illegitimate coins has never been determined. Some believe it may have been as late as 1918. The majority contend that the surreptitious minting must have happened in late 1912, before the release of James Earle Fraser's Indian Head nickel.

Noted researcher R.W. Julian, who had access to Mint documents subsequently destroyed, has effectively argued the latter theory — claiming that if the coins were struck prior to the release of the Indian Head nickel, the striking would have to have taken place sometime following the December 1912 order to change to James Earle Fraser's Indian Head nickel design and before a general defacement of outdated dies at year's end. Julian was able to substantiate the existence of 1913-dated Liberty Head nickel dies through records of a shipment to the San Francisco Mint. The shipment was made prior to the decision to change to the Indian Head nickel design. [1]

Others, however, point to the lapse of time between 1913, the year the Indian Head nickel was released, and Brown's 1920 visit to the ANA convention as being suspect. They contend that the coins could have been produced much later than 1913, perhaps by a Mint guard rumored to have been let go in 1918 under mysterious circumstances.

A cash offer

Hobbyists apparently first learned of the possible existence of a 1913-dated Liberty Head nickel through the December 1919 issue of *The Numismatist*, where Brown offered to pay $500 in cash for an example, "in Proof condition, if possible." He ran a similar advertisement in the January 1920 issue, upping his offer to $600 per coin.

On Monday, Aug. 23, 1920, he attended the opening day of the American Numismatic Association's four-day convention in Chicago, where he displayed at least one example of the 1913 Liberty Head nickel and told of the existence of five such coins. The October 1920 issue of *The Numismatist* notes:

> "Samuel W. Brown of North Tonawanda, N.Y., was present for a short time on Monday. He had with him a specimen of the latest great rarity in U.S. coinage — the nickel of 1913 of the Liberty Head type. It was among the exhibits the remainder of the Convention, with a label announcing that it was valued at $600, which amount Mr. Brown announced he is ready to pay for all proof specimens offered to him." [2]

Brown explained that at the close of 1912 the Mint had not yet received orders to use the Indian Head nickel dies, and had prepared a "master die" of the Liberty Head design, dated 1913. From this master die, Brown said, a few specimens were struck, "believed to be five," in proof, none of which were

Brown first offered to pay $500 for examples of the 1913 Liberty Head nickel. He later upped the ante to $600. In 1920 he attended the American Numismatic Association convention in Chicago where he displayed an example of the rarity. Courtesy of The Numismatist.

thought to have been placed into circulation.

Upon his departure from the convention, Brown left the coin in the care of Chicago Coin Club president Alden Scott Boyer. It was placed on display until Aug. 26, 1920, the date the convention closed.

A few months later, Brown requested that Boyer return the nickel, as a sale was pending. Brown wrote:

> "Dear Mr. Boyer — I would appreciate it very much if you would return the 1913 Liberty head nickel you have with your coins in the Masonic Temple vault in your city. I have a deal pending for the sale of this coin, and it is necessary that I have it within the next ten days. If you will, kindly send it to me express, charges collect, and estimate the value at $750. Thanking you for your courtesy in this matter." [3]

Thus, according to the most widely accepted theory, Brown had created an artificial rarity, developed a market for the coin, and eventually sold one or all five specimens.

A clever ruse

Who was Samuel Brown? How did he gain access to the Mint? Where did he obtain an appreciation for coins as being rare and collectible?

The answers to these questions — important in determining Brown's role in the story — were supplied by Don Taxay, who discovered that Brown had been employed by the Philadelphia Mint as an assistant curator of its coin cabinet from 1904 to 1907 and as a clerk/storekeeper until he left the Mint's employ in 1913. In 1906, Brown joined the ANA.

Supposition holds that Brown, with his knowledge of coin collecting (gained through his ANA membership and term as assistant curator at the Mint), was most culpable in the creation of the 1913 Liberty Head nickel. His advertisements in *The Numismatist*, it is said, were only a clever ruse, that when he arrived at the ANA convention he already had all five coins with him. (Some writers go so far as to add the colorful notation that he brought the coins to the convention in a special holder, but there is no proof of this. Such a holder exists, but its origin is unclear.)

Unfortunately, no written record apparently exists proving that Brown had all five coins *at* the convention, that he knew of their lo-

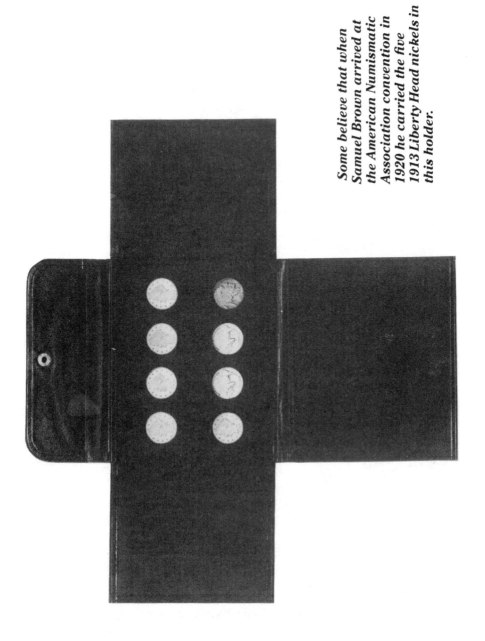

Some believe that when Samuel Brown arrived at the American Numismatic Association convention in 1920 he carried the five 1913 Liberty Head nickels in this holder.

cation, or that he already possessed all five. That Brown knew of the existence of five specimens is obvious from the reference in the October 1920 issue of *The Numismatist*. But despite what countless writers have said, only one specimen has truly been accounted for as being at the convention.

The difference is, at first glance, a minor one. Brown may, after all, have had possession of the other four coins and simply failed to bring the complete set to the convention. Or, less likely, the editor of *The Numismatist* failed to correctly identify the number of 1913 Liberty Head nickels on display.

But the possibility exists that Brown's ads in *The Numismatist* were not a complete hoax, that knowing of the existence of other 1913 Liberty Head nickels, either because he was involved in or simply aware of the striking, Brown was genuinely hoping to obtain the remaining specimens before anyone else did.

Guilt by association

The point to remember when assessing the damning charges consistently leveled against Brown is that the case against him is based primarily on circumstantial evidence. Playing the same game, one can easily paint an entirely different picture of Brown and his activities in relation to these unauthorized rarities.

In his article, "Coin of Chance, Coin of Change, Coin of Conspiracy," in the May 1975 issue of *Coins* magazine, Julian made the reasonable observation that Brown couldn't have been alone in the production of these illegitimate coins. He wrote:

> "The person responsible for actually striking the 1913 liberty head nickels almost certainly was in the engraver's department or an employee of the medal room itself, with the latter being the best bet. There were at least two men in on the plot, because the man who sold them some years later [Brown], although a former mint employee, did not work in the key area required for access to the proof dies." [4]

The striking, Julian argues, must have occurred within a few days of Dec. 16, 1912, the date orders went out to the San Francisco Mint to return the 1913-dated dies sent to that mint in November 1912.

"The conspirators surely knew that the 1913 liberty head dies were liable for return to the engraver's department for destruction at any moment, and no time was to be lost if they were to have the only such coins," Julian wrote. [5]

If Julian's contention is correct — if Brown was involved in striking the coins he must had an accomplice — it could just as easily be suggested that Brown may not have obtained *all* of the specimens upon leaving the Mint. Wouldn't his co-conspirator have wanted to keep one or more of the coins?

Model citizen

Using circumstantial evidence it could also be argued that Brown's "model citizen" life after leaving the Mint proves he was totally above such chicanery, an honored and respected citizen who has been wrongly indicted, tried, convicted and sentenced by the numismatic community without due process.

Reporting on Brown's death, the August 1944 issue of *The Numismatist* told that Brown, a native of Pennsylvania, served several terms as mayor of North Tonawanda, N.Y., spent 10 years on the board of education, and once served on the U.S. Assay Commission. [6]

An obituary notice in the June 19, 1944, issue of the North Tonawanda *Evening News* adds additional biographical information on Brown. Noting that Brown (age 64 at the time of his death) was a Republican, the *News* said Brown served as mayor of North Tonawanda from 1932-1933, having moved to that city in 1913 to go into association with Wayne Fahnestock in Frontier Chocolate Co. Later Brown was employed by Pierce-Brown Co., retiring in 1924.

Brown was a member of Sutherland Lodge No. 826, of the Free and Accepted Masons, of which he was past master. He also served as district deputy grandmaster of the Niagara Oleans district and was a member of the Buffalo consistory, the Ismailia Temple and the Shrine Club of Tonawanda. [7]

Do these sound like the credentials of a nefarious character? Of course not. Does it prove that Brown was innocent of the charges numismatists have made against him? No, it doesn't. The point is, Brown has been convicted by association, not on the basis of hard facts.

It's a charge that will likely stick, even though what really happened may never be known. Left to the fertile imaginations of those who look for nefarious motives in every human action, the story will continue to be a murky mirror of the truth at best.

Fit for a king

By 1924 all five specimens of the 1913 Liberty Head nickel had come into August Wagner's possession. An ad by Wagner in the December 1923 issue advised:

> "FOR SALE. Five (5) Liberty Head 1913 Coins. Proof. The only Five-Cent Liberty Head Coins of this design and year in existence."

The coins then passed through various hands to the eccentric Col. E.H.R. Green, who readily lavished money on his collectibles. Born in London on Aug. 22, 1868, Green was the son of Edward Howland Robinson Green. He was raised, however, by his wealthy mother, Hetty Green, whose miserly ways came to the fore when her son injured his leg in a sledding accident at the age of 9. Legend has it, she refused to call a doctor, preferring to save money by treating his injury herself.

Two years later, when he re-injured the leg, she dressed the boy in rags and took him from free clinic to free clinic. When a doctor found out who she was and demanded payment, she refused. Some years later, the leg had to be amputated.

As much as his mother liked to squirrel money away, her son enjoyed spending it. According to Arthur H. Lewis in *The Day They Shook the Plum Tree*, the 6-foot 4-inch, 300-pound Green spent nearly $3 million a year on yachts, coins, stamps, jewels and other dalliances.

In a mimic of a successful sales promotion by Texas coin dealer B. Max Mehl, Green once offered $10,000 for anyone discovering an additional 1913 Liberty Head nickel. It was a reward he knew full well would never have to be paid. [8]

Mehl had already made the rarity famous through a series of radio and press promotions, offering to pay $50 for anyone discovering a new 1913 Liberty Head nickel. The gimmick paid off in new clients for his rare coin business but not in new nickels.

Following Green's death, in 1936, the coins next came into the possession of either dealer Burdette Johnson or collector Eric P. Newman. The exact ownership details are a bit foggy. Although Johnson is generally credited as being the next in line to receive all five coins, Newman said in an interview with this writer that he once owned all of the coins. The June 1961 issue of *Numismatic Scrapbook Magazine* notes similarly that "before the late B.G. Johnson split up the set in the Green estate, Eric P. Newman had all specimens in his possession . . ." [9]

Newman kept at least one specimen, which later went to dealer Abe Kosoff and found its way to Ambassador R. Henry Norweb and

Texas coin dealer B. Max Mehl helped make the 1913 Liberty Head nickel famous through a promotion offering to pay a reward for additional specimens. The reward did nothing to bring out new specimens. It served primarily to promote his rare coin business.

his wife. It currently resides in the collection of the Smithsonian Institution.

At one point two specimens were owned by Egypt's playboy ruler, King Farouk. According to Kosoff, who chronicled the sale of the king's collection in a series of articles for *Coin World*, Farouk (whose extravagances ran from sex to gambling to eclectic collections) obtained the Fred C. Boyd specimen of the rarity from Kosoff and had, at about the same time, placed a successful bid for a different example in Mehl's sale of the Fred Olsen collection. [10]

According to Kosoff, Farouk commissioned Mehl to sell the additional specimen. When Farouk abdicated in 1952, the royal collection was put up for sale. The sale, held two years later, was the landmark numismatic event of its day, with many prominent dealers and numismatists making the trip to Egypt to bid on the collection's extensive U.S. holdings. The 1913 Liberty Head nickel went for just under $4,000. [11]

Another specimen was apparently last seen with dealer George O. Walton and some believe may have been lost in 1962 when Walton was killed while traveling to a coin show in Wilson, N.C. Others, however, question whether or not Walton ever owned a genuine example of the coin.

This "missing" specimen became the topic of a wave of numismatic press inquiries into its whereabouts in 1993 and a reward *a la* Mehl for its recovery. Despite the reward, the location of this specimen remains a mystery.

MacNickel

The most colorful and endearing owner of a 1913 Liberty Head was J.V. McDermott, a hard drinking, vest-pocket dealer from Milwaukee who was known for sliding "MacNickel" down the bar for the curious to see. McDermott purchased his specimen of the 1913 Liberty Head nickel from Jim Kelly in the early 1940s for $900 and quickly made himself and the nickel famous.

Even today, many numismatists have cherished stories to tell of their meetings with McDermott and of his rare nickel. Such is the case with collector Tom Fruit, who as a child became a friend and sometimes caretaker of the famous coin.

Fruit, 14 at the time, met McDermott in 1949 after Fruit's family moved to the south part of Milwaukee. A coin collector, Fruit became intrigued when he learned that a famous coin dealer lived not too far from his house. He went right over and knocked on the back door, where he was greeted by McDermott, clad in a sleeveless T-shirt.

"He was really nice," Fruit said. "I told him I was interested in collecting coins, so he reached into his pocket and pulled out a Pine Tree Shilling and his 1913 nickel." [12]

Fruit became a regular patron of McDermott's, going back to make purchases from the dealer whenever a spare $5 or $10 earned from an odd job allowed.

For a young collector, the association was a dream come true — a wealth of coins only a few feet from his family's home. The two became friends. When Fruit turned 16 and was able to drive, he often drove McDermott to coin club meetings and coin shows.

"He would drive there and I'd drive back, because he did most of his business at the bar," Fruit said of McDermott. "He never had a table that I remember. His table was the bar."

McDermott made no secret of his passion for drinking, and often made reference to it at the beginning of his advertisements in *Numismatic Scrapbook Magazine*. In the February 1950 issue he said: "Had a bad cold last month. Doc says, 'Go to bed for a couple of days.' But I didn't[,] as long as I can lift my arm and bend an elbow. I['ll] never give up."

From the February 1954 issue came: "That Dan Brown guy out in Denver told me of a rumor that's goin' around to whit that they're goin' to make us eat our corn instead of drink it — it's very disturbing."

And from the September 1960 issue: "Had to miss the Boston show — my neck looked like a hunk of raw meat (reaction from those x-ray treatments I guess). Looks like I'll have some surgery. Oh! Me! Some of my

Dealer J.V. McDermott in what is likely a rare photograph of the popular dealer at a bourse table. He was said to have conducted most of his coin deals at the bar and made no secret of his passion for a good drink.

Two owners of the famous "MacNickel." J.V. McDermott, at left, and Aubrey Bebee. The coin is now owned

*by the
American
Numismatic
Association,
having been
donated to
the non-profit
organization
by the Bebees.*

pals want to get a pool going and one tavern-keeper has offered to mount my head behind his bar. (He says — as a warning to others.) Another one says he thinks it would be better if they shrink it. Anyway, I may fool them if lucky."

Fruit remembers taking the famous coin to school to have pictures taken for McDermott.

"I used to carry that nickel around for days at a time," he said. "I'd carry it around in my pocket. He wasn't afraid to give it to anybody.

"A lot of times, at a coin show, he didn't know where it was. It would be circulated up and down the bar and somebody would have it. Anytime I wanted the nickel, he would just give it to me. He didn't ask any questions."

Collector Walter Walters also remembers seeing McDermott and his famous nickel. One day in 1948 Walters' father, who was tending bar, gave young Walters two Mercury dimes and asked McDermott, a bar patron, to show him his nickel.

"He [McDermott] had it in his wallet with a snap pocket, nothing else," Walters said. "He just told me it was worth a lot and [there] were only a few around.

"I was only 14 and wasn't into coins very much, but I saved all the Liberty nickels for the next three years."

McDermott also freely loaned the coin to clubs to promote their coin shows. Some believe, however, that with the number of venues at which the coin appeared, McDermott must have had a duplicate made. Fruit discounts such stories.

"There was a lot of talk that Mac had the real nickel and then a replica of it, and that is not true," he said. "There has never been any substantiation to that.

"In fact, I know it is not true, because I could recognize that nickel today. It had a little dent or flake missing right underneath the [Liberty's] jaw. So I could recognize that nickel anytime, and it was always the same nickel.

"I think the reason for that is, people thought that he would never let a coin that expensive out of his sight. But that didn't bother him because, he said, 'What good is it to anybody. Everybody knows where the five nickels are and everybody knows that there are only five. Any one that would turn up, if it was stolen, nobody could sell it, because they would know whose it was.' So that is why he really wasn't concerned about anybody swiping it, and nobody ever did."

Even after Fruit moved away from Milwaukee he found that McDermott was willing to loan him the coin (at that point valued at nearly $12,500) for display at coin shows.

McDermott's attitude toward loaning his valuable coin out for others to enjoy can be seen in an article he wrote for *Coins* magazine shortly before his death.

"I don't believe this coin, or any rarity, should be perpetually consigned to the concealing darkness of a bank vault," McDermott said. "Legally one man may 'own' this 1913 Liberty head nickel, but in a very real sense it belongs to numismatics; for should the collecting fraternity lose interest in it the 1913 would fall by the wayside — all five would be required to buy a handi-pack of not-so-good five cent cigars." [13]

McDermott died on Sept. 29, 1966. The obituary notice in *The Numismatist* said, "He had myriad friends but few, if any, intimates," but he "will live long in the memory of many who saw him and 'it' from coast to coast." [14]

Up for bid

Following her husband's death, McDermott's wife, Elizabeth, consigned the coin to a sale held Aug. 8, 1967, during the ANA convention in Miami, where it was cataloged by auctioneer James Kelly as lot 2214.

Aubrey and Adeline Bebee at the 1967 sale of the McDermott specimen of the 1913 Liberty Head nickel.

Thanks to an audiotape made by Charles Hoskins, Kelly's call of the sale of this famous coin was recorded for posterity.

"I think we are approaching [a] moment that is going to be something to remember in the history of numismatics," auctioneer Jim Kelly said as he announced the sale of the 1913 Liberty Head nickel.

After introducing the lot to the gathered bidders, Kelly said, "I hope this goes down in history as one of the outstanding sales in the country . . . and you have the coin."

The nickel was then brought to Kelly, who held it up nervously for photographers.

"I will try to hold it steady, maybe," he said.

After a pause, Kelly mistakenly announced, "Ladies and Gentlemen, we are going to start the bidding on the 1931 nickel." He gracefully covered his mistake saying, "You know that would be more rare than the 1913 nickel, because they didn't make a '31.

"It would be even more rare than the '13. We're starting the bidding tonight on the 1913 nickel . . . I have $38,000. Can I hear 40,000?"

At that point Nebraska dealer Aubrey Bebee placed a bid.

Aubrey Bebee following his successful purchase of McDermott's 1913 Liberty Head nickel. Elizabeth McDermott is second from left. Also shown are auctioneer Jim Kelly and Adeline Bebee.

Like McDermott, Bebee regularly displayed the 1913 Liberty Head nickel at coin shows and conventions.

"I have 40,000, can I get 42?" Julian Marks then bid $42,000. "I have 42, can I get 44?" Kelly queried, "I have 42 here, can I get 44? It's here at 42, can I get 44?"

Bebee responded at $44,000.

"I have 44, can I get 46?" Kelly asked. "I have 44,000, can I get 46?

"I have 44,000, can I get 46? 44,000 I have, can I get 46? The count is done at 44,000, can I get 46,000?"

"That's my bid, Jim," Bebee answered.

"44,000 is your bid," Kelly acknowledged, "Can I get 46?" "44, can I get 46? It will be too late tomorrow to change your mind. To anyone interested now's the time to — because it's the last chance. I have 44,000, can I hear 46,000? Can I hear 45,000? I have 44, can I get 45,000?"

Kosoff then entered a bid.

"I have 45,000 now, can I get 46?" Kelly asked. "I have 45, you got 46?"

Bebee bid at $46,000.

"I have now, 7," Kelly says. "I have 46, can I get 47? I have 46,000, can I get 47?

"It's your bid at 46,000, can I get 47? It's at 46, can I get 47? The bid is at $46,000, can I get 47,000? Can I get 46,500? 46,500? That's as low as we go. It's 46,500, 46,500.

"It's still cheap at 46,500 with $50,000 in publicity — 46,500. I have the 46,000, can I get the 500?"

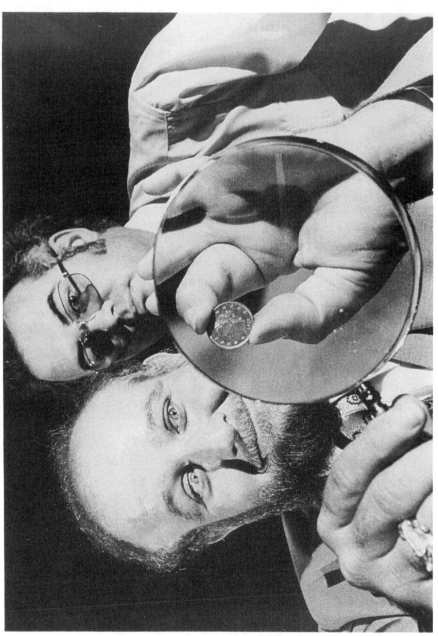

Collector Reed Hawn at the October 1993 sale of his 1913 Liberty Head nickel. The coin sold for just shy of $1 million, at $962,500. **Photo courtesy of Stack's.**

Responding to an anxious bidder, Kelly said, "We're going to start 'em in a minute or two, we don't want to hurry you, we want you to make up your mind. Don't be hasty.

"I have 46,000, can I get the 500? 46,000, I'll take 500. Are you all done at 46,000, $46,000? In a minute now it will be too late. This is the time now to make up your mind. I have $46,000. $46,000.

I have $46,000 once. $46,0000 twice. For the third and last time, I have $46,000. Sold to Mr. Bebee at $46,000."

Applause broke out for Bebee and the auction halted so that pictures could be taken. It was, as Kelly said, an important moment in numismatic history.

Bebee and his wife, Adeline, would gain much favorable notice over the years for their record-breaking purchase. They later donated their specimen to the ANA Money Museum, where it resides today.

Just shy of $1 million

On Oct. 13, 1993, excitement over the sale of a 1913 Liberty Head nickel stirred once again as Texas millionaire Reed Hawn's example crossed the block in New York. Hawn purchased his 1913 Liberty Head nickel from Superior Galleries' January 1985 sale of the Dr. Jerry Buss collection, where it was graded Proof-63, and brought a record $385,000. That was the last time, prior to the 1993 sale, that a 1913 Liberty Head nickel had appeared at public auction.

This coin's pedigree traced through the Farouk collection and was featured in an episode of *Hawaii Five-O*, where it was held admiringly before the television camera by guest star Victor Buono.

Bidding opened strong and climbed quickly to the $700,000 mark, with several bidders still active. When all was said and done, the 1913 Liberty Head nickel had entered the realm of elite among U.S. coin rarities — bringing a hammer price of $875,000, a total of $962,500 including the 10 percent buyer's fee.

It was a big price for a small coin with an uncertain past but a million-dollar future.

Chapter 4

An unsinkable coin

Of shipwrecks, high seas adventure and rare, missing dollars

Shipwrecks are a popular source of riches for today's treasure hunter. They should also be a popular source for 1804 silver dollars, if you believe the rumors circulated for years as explanation for this coin being a great U.S. rarity.

Though not the only coin ever touted as having come by its rarity via its mintage being vanquished to Davy Jones's locker, the 1804 dollar is one of the most famous and valuable of U.S. coins, bringing with it tall tales fit for any swashbuckler worth his sea salt.

Creating a rarity

Coinage of the silver dollar began at the U.S. Mint in 1794, but mis-calculations as to the proper weight for the coin caused the coins to disappear from circulation soon after release.

A depositor at the first Mint could make a profit at the Mint's expense by sending the coins to the West Indies. There, the lighter-weight U.S. silver dollars were traded at par for the heavier Spanish or Mexican silver eight-reales, which were shipped back to the United States for recoinage. As a result, few early U.S. silver dollars entered circulation; most were melted.

The same story was basically true for the nation's early gold coinage. The bimetallic ratio set by the United States, by which silver traded for gold, was at first off the mark in relation to world ratios.

Miscalculations in the proper weight for the U.S. silver dollar, first struck in 1794, led the coins to be produced primarily for export. Few entered circulation, causing President Thomas Jefferson to order a halt to coinage.

Although dated 1804, no silver dollars were struck in that year. The first of the 1804 silver dollars were produced in the 1830s, with later strikings bringing the number known to 15. The piece shown is the Class I Dexter specimen.

This meant that gold coins either disappeared shortly after minting or languished in bank vaults.

It is generally agreed today that no U.S. silver dollars dated 1804 were struck in that year, coinage having been halted because of the inability to keep the coins in circulation. The same is true of existing 1804-dated gold eagles.

Landmark research by Eric P. Newman and Kenneth E. Bressett, presented in their 1962 book *The Fantastic 1804 Silver Dollar*, has convinced numismatists that the 19,570 silver dollars recorded by the Mint as being struck in 1804 were actually dated 1803. Further, that the first-known examples of 1804-dated silver dollars (Class I) were minted in the 1830s for inclusion in special presentation sets to be given to foreign dignitaries. Additional strikings were made surreptitiously through the latter part of the 19th century. Today the count stands at 15 genuine examples known and hundreds, if not thousands, of fakes.

Seaworthy tales

Until the Newman and Bressett book, numismatists were informally divided into two groups — those who believed existing 1804 dollars were struck in 1804 and those who thought the coins were of later manufacture.

To explain how these coins could have been minted in 1804 and yet the majority of mintage lost, several tales of high seas adventure surfaced. One of the more spirited was tied to the Barbary Coast pirates.

Under this history-soaked tale, the coins went to a watery grave aboard the U.S. frigate *Philadelphia*. The frigate was set aflame in February 1804 by Navy Lieutenant Stephen Decatur, who heroically sailed the ketch *Intrepid* into the Tripoli harbor to keep the *Philadelphia* out of the hands of the Tripolitanians. Most of the 1804 dollar and half-dollar mintage went down, like any good captain, with the ship.

Newman and Bressett tell an additional Tripoli-related tale, by which, in 1804 an expedition was led from the United States against Tripoli, headed by Capt. William Eaton and Hamet Carmanly, the exiled brother of the bashaw of Tripoli. After 15 days of torturous marching across thousands of miles of searing desert, they accomplished their mission. The 1804 silver dollars were shipped to the coast of Africa to pay the brave men. Few of the rare dollars ever returned to this country. [1]

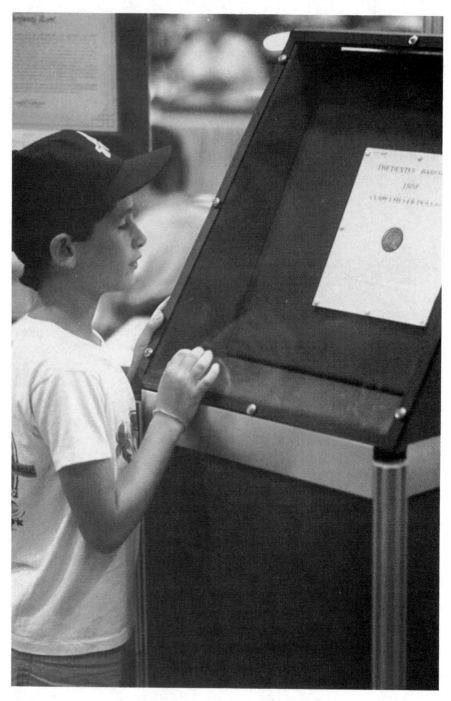

Although priced well out of the range of most collectors, show goers often get a chance to get a close up look at the "King of American coins." Photo by Roger Case.

Oriental misadventure

Yet another seagoing theory placed the coins in an iron chest aboard a merchantman bound for a U.S. frigate in Oriental waters. The victim of a typhoon, the merchantman and its precious cargo went to the bottom of the stormy sea. [2]

In a differing version, by which all but a few of 1804 dollars "now lie at the bottom of the Pacific ocean somewhere between Cape Horn and Hong-Kong," religious zealots were blamed. Apparently a Huguenot employed at the Mint was the culprit. He became incensed by the portrait on the silver dollar, believing it bore too close a resemblance to First Lady Martha Washington. He let the word out to others and Huguenots throughout the nation "set up a hue and cry against having the picture of any ruler or nay member of any ruler's or former ruler's family on the money. As a result, not one of the coins was sent from the mint for general distribution. A few of them afterward were traded by the mint for perfect specimens of coins that were not in the mint cabinet, and that accounts for the fact that just a few of them are in the hands of coin collectors." [3]

Land-based theories

Land-based theories for the disappearance of the 1804 silver dollars were also generously provided. One of the more plausible asserted that the high price of silver caused the melting of most of the coinage. Another accounted for the low number of known examples by suggesting that the Mint had supplied just enough silver for 10 or 12 of the coins to be struck. [4]

Yet another theory, advanced by Robert E. Preston, U.S. Mint director 1893-1898, proclaimed that the entire mintage had been sent to Central America and only a few drifted back into this country. [5]

Plenty of fakes

Ever since pioneer U.S. coin collector Matthew Stickney obtained an 1804 silver dollar in trade at the U.S. Mint in 1843, the 1804 silver dollar has been popular among collectors and perhaps even more popular with counterfeiters looking to make a quick buck. In the mid-1800s the nation's tavern keepers were targets for the unscrupulous, who fobbed off altered 1800-dated dollars as 1804 dollars.

B.H. Collins, described as having been associated with the U.S.

Unlike the 1804 silver dollar, a small amount of 1804-dated gold $10 eagles were struck before the official order came to halt eagle and silver dollar coinage. Like the 1804 silver dollar, a limited number of 1804-dated gold eagles were produced in the 1830s for inclusion in diplomatic presentation sets. Only four of these "plain 4" proofs are known.

Treasury for years, recorded in the March 1899 issue of *The Numis-matist* that the bogus rarities were manufactured by a man named Kennedy in Lowell, Mass., who took 1800-dated dollars, removed the final "0," "covered the face [of the coin] with wax, etched a figure 4 in the proper place" and, with the use of a galvanic battery, at-tached the new digit in such a means that it "endured all the texts known to numismatics."

The newly created 1804 dollars were then distributed by tramps in his employ, "who claimed to have inherited fortunes and wasted them in dissipation, with the exception of one valuable coin, which was worth thousands of dollars." [6] With genuine 1804 silver dollars bringing in the range of $600 in the 1870s, it was likely a lucrative business.

Since the turn of the century the population of known examples would at first glance appear to have grown considerably, as journals devoted to numismatics have been littered with references to so-called "discoveries" of additional 1804 silver dollars. Most of these reports were ill-based. A few more examples turned up this century, raising the count of genuine examples of the three identified classes to a mere 15 pieces.

Today it would take a king's ransom to purchase an example of the "King of American Coins," the unsinkable 1804 silver dollar.

Chapter 5

An indecent coin

Was public outcry against the nudity on the Standing Liberty quarter the real reason for the design change?

An age-old hobby story tells that when Hermon MacNeil's beautiful Standing Liberty quarter was released, the public was outraged. Offended by the blatant display of partial nudity on the coin's figure of Liberty, Americans rose up in protest over the new quarter, causing the Mint to bring coinage to a halt and replace the risque design with a more demure, fully clothed Liberty.

But is this really the truth behind the creation of this now popular and sought-after coin?

MacNeil, the artist

It is perhaps ironic that a man who once served as president of National Sculpture Society — and was awarded medals for his life-size sculptures at expositions in Chicago; Buffalo, N.Y.; Paris; and Charleston, S.C. — should be remembered by numismatists almost exclusively for his design on the Standing Liberty quarter and the controversy supposedly surrounding it depicting Liberty with her right breast exposed.

A vintage hobby tale contends that, when the Standing Liberty quarter was released in 1916, public outcry against the partial nudity on the figure of Liberty led to a halt in coinage early the following year. The design was then changed to feature a chain-mail covering over Liberty's upper torso. Records would seem to indicate, however, that the story was largely a myth. Not only was there no great surge of complaints from the public about the first design, artist Hermon MacNeil likely preferred the switch to the chain-mail design.

Hermon A. MacNeil was the product of an era in which artists were encouraged to display their creations at major world expositions, including the 1893 World's Columbian Exposition in Chicago.

MacNeil, born near Chelsea, Mass., on Feb. 27, 1866, to John Clinton MacNeil and Mary (Lash) MacNeil, was the product of a new age in American sculpture. It was an age in which sculpture gained equal status with other forms of art and was considered by many to be on par with architecture.

He participated in a fruitful era of great expositions that allowed young sculptors — including Augustus Saint-Gaudens, Adolph Weinman, James Earle Fraser, John Flanagan, and Victor D. Brenner — a rich creative forum for their artistic endeavors.

Expositions such as the World Columbian Exposition in 1893, the Paris Exposition in 1900, the Pan-American Exposition in 1901, the Louisiana Purchase Exposition in 1904, and the Pan-Pacific Exposition in 1915 were eagerly sought out by artists looking to showcase their talents to the world.

As a youngster, MacNeil attended public schools in Chelsea, where his artistic talents began to blossom and were encouraged. At the urging of his cousin, Jeanette Mitchell, MacNeil entered Massachusetts State Normal Art School. He completed the four-year course, graduating in 1886 with highest honors.

For the next three years he taught industrial arts at Sibley College — the former name for Cornell University's School of Engineering.

In 1888, at the urging of Sibley's dean, Robert H. Thurston, who recognized MacNeil's artistic and modeling abilities, MacNeil borrowed $500 from his uncle and went to Paris, where he pursued his career in sculpture.

Paris, at the time of MacNeil's arrival, was considered the artistic center for sculptors. American sculptors flocked there to study in the ateliers of the great French sculptors, and MacNeil gladly joined them.

MacNeil studied for three years at the Academie Julian under the tutelage of Henry Chapu and at the Ecole des Beaux-Arts, where his teacher was the renowned Jean Falguire. MacNeil absorbed much of the impressionistic modeling of the French school, and its influence remained evident throughout his career.

In 1891 he returned to New York, where he obtained a letter of introduction from Saint-Gaudens to Philip Martiny. Martiny was involved in preparing the sculptural decorations for the World Columbian Exposition being held in Chicago. MacNeil worked with Martiny and also created two figures of his own design for the Electricity Building at the exposition.

Following the exposition, MacNeil remained in Chicago, where he secured a position teaching modeling during the evenings at the school of the Chicago Art Institute. During the day, he worked on various sculptural projects, including four bas-reliefs of Pere Marquette for the Marquette Building in Chicago. The scenes depict the Jesuit priest's life among the Indians in the early days of the settlement of Chicago.

MacNeil was fascinated by the American Indian — a theme that would occupy the majority of his sculptural efforts for the next decade. He studied their life-styles, customs and ceremonies.

In 1895 he took an extensive trip to America's Southwest, traveling through Colorado, Arizona and New Mexico, where he studied the life of the Moquis and Zunis tribes, from which he created several statues.

At summer's end MacNeil was invited to submit photographs of his works in competition for the Rinehart Scholarship to study in Rome. He won the award and, before leaving for Rome, married one of his students, Carol L. Brooks, a sculptor, who is best remembered artistically for her work *Foolish Virgin*.

The scholarship was originally to last only one year, but it was extended. MacNeil and his wife spent 1896 to 1900 in Rome.

To meet the scholarship requirements, MacNeil had to create several sculptures. Notable among his works were the bust *Agnese Mattelia* and the sculptures *A Primitive Chant* (modeled after Black Pipe, a destitute Indian he had met in Chicago), *From Chaos Came Light* and *Sun Vow*.

Sun Vow, an enlargement of a sketch he made in Chicago, was apparently inspired by the Sioux Indian nation's initiation ceremony. It depicts an Indian sitting at the side of his adolescent boy, who has just shot an arrow toward the sun.

Another work, *Moqui Runner*, is a bronze statuette of an Indian dashing across the desert with a tangle of serpents in his hands — reminiscent of a Prayer for Rain ceremony, which MacNeil had occasion to observe on his trip to America's Southwest.

In 1899 MacNeil closed his studio at the Villa dell' Aurora and went to Paris for a year, where he worked on the decorations for the U.S. building at the Paris Exposition.

At the Paris Exposition, two of MacNeil's studies, *Sun Vow* and *Moqui Runner*, were to bring critical acclaim.

Sun Vow won a silver medal in Paris and a year later earned its creator a gold medal at the Pan-American Exposition in Buffalo. It was also exhibited at the Louisiana Purchase Exposition in St. Louis in 1904.

Sun Vow was held in such high esteem that Lorado Taft, in his 1930 *History of American Sculpture*, said, "This group is good enough and important enough to assure its author a permanent place in the history of American art."

By the time he returned to New York to establish a studio, MacNeil was already a respected sculptor. Just prior to his return, a special showing of several of his pieces was held in 1899 at New York's esteemed Metropolitan Museum of Art.

After his return, he was asked to do the pedimental decoration for the Anthropological Building at the Pan-American Exposition and a sculptural group, *Despotic Age*, which stood in front of the U.S. government building. His work *Agnese Mattelia*, created in Rome, and another work, *Beatrice*, were also displayed.

MacNeil was also commissioned to design the exposition's official gold award medal. The medal depicts a youthful woman standing beside a buffalo — representing the triumph of intellect over physical power. On the reverse, a North American Indian offers a peace pipe to a South American Indian.

MacNeil also created sculptural pieces for an exposition in Charleston. An exhibit at the Pratt Institute in Brooklyn, N.Y., had 22 of MacNeil's works, 17 of which were on Indian subjects.

For the Louisiana Purchase Exposition in 1904, his sculptural work included an Indian boy running beside a buffalo. For Portland, Ore., he modeled *The Coming of the White Man*.

In 1910 his sculptural work devoted to the Indian was just about ended. For the Panama-Pacific Exposition in 1915, he modeled signs of the zodiac in stylized forms related to abstract art.

Other notable works by MacNeil include the *McKinley Memorial* in Columbus, Ohio; a statute of Ezra Cornell on the campus of Cornell University in Ithaca, N.Y; the *Judge Burke Memorial* in Seattle; a portrait of Judge Ellsworth in Hartford, Conn.; and a bronze figure of Gen. George Rogers Clark in Vincennes, Ind.

He created a statue of George Washington for the Washington Arch in New York City; a Pilgrim fathers-and-mothers group in Waterbury, Conn.; a statue of Marquette for Chicago's West Park; a soldiers-and-sailors monument in Albany, N.Y.; *Defenders of Fort Sumter* in Charleston, S.C.; a marble pedimental group for the Supreme Court Building in Washington, D.C.; and a 130-foot-long bas-relief frieze for the Missouri State Capitol.

A small but important work

It is, therefore, readily apparent that in terms of physical size, MacNeil's much-acclaimed Standing Liberty quarter was the smallest of his works. In relation to numismatics and its place in U.S. coinage history, it is, however, one of his most important and the most beautiful.

Three letters obtained by coin dealer Michael C. Annis in 1987 formed the basis of an article by this writer in a 1988 issue of *Coins* magazine, which explored the background of the artist and re-examined the story behind the quarter's release, leading to the conclusion that the design change in 1917 was not due to public protest over nudity on the Type I quarter. [1]

The letters in question came from the estate of Cecilia W. (Muench) MacNeil, whom MacNeil married in 1946, following the death of his first wife, two years prior.

The first letter, dated Oct. 26, 1900, is a handwritten introduction from Henry Mitchell, a gem and seal engraver from Boston, to a Mr. Tiffe in Buffalo.

The letter introduces Mitchell's nephew, MacNeil, "of whom I spoke when I had the pleasure of calling upon you at Marlboro." It continues, "He [MacNeil] has just written me that he was about to go to your City on business connected with the Exposition."

This interesting letter was apparently written in connection with the Pan-American Exposition and may have in some way been tied to MacNeil's work on the medal for that exposition.

Mitchell is, in all likelihood, the uncle who generously loaned the young sculptor the $500 he needed to pursue his studies in Paris. Mitchell's daughter, Jeanette Mitchell, as has been previously observed, is said to have encouraged the young artist to attend the Massachusetts State Normal Art School.

The letter was written on Mitchell's personalized stationery, which advised, "Medal Dies Engraved and Medals Struck in Gold, Silver and Bronze."

Mitchell, the son of sculptor F.N. Mitchell, was a prominent medalist of the period. His medallic works are strewn throughout R.W. Julian's *Medals of the United States Mint: The First Century 1792-1892.* One of Mitchell's most important works was an award medal for the U.S. Centennial in 1876.

Mitchell was so highly regarded that, according to Q. David Bowers in *The History of United States Coinage: As Illustrated by the Garrett Collection*, when the Treasury Department proposed design changes in 1890, Mitchell was included among possible design-competition judges along with Saint-Gaudens and Charles Barber.

A letter of introduction from Mitchell must have, therefore, carried considerable weight, and one can readily assume that MacNeil put it to good use.

The second letter held by Annis, and the most significant in relation to the Standing Liberty quarter design, was a notification of the Treasury Department's acceptance of MacNeil's design.

Dated May 23, 1916, this typewritten letter, on the Mint director's official stationery, was signed by Mint Director R.W. Woolley and Treasury Secretary William G. McAdoo. It read, "It gives me great pleasure to notify you formally that the designs submitted by you for the proposed new Quarter Dollar have been accepted, and are hereby approved."

An unsigned copy of this letter (but on stationery headed by the words "Treasury Department") appears in J.H. Cline's *Standing Liberty Quarters*. Cline also reproduced several other important letters that help to piece together the history of MacNeil's quarter.

In 1915 MacNeil was selected along with Weinman and one other artist from a field of 50 entrants to submit designs for the redesign of the nation's subsidiary silver coinage.

MacNeil was notified of his selection — along with Weinman and an artist name Polasek — by a letter from Woolley dated Dec. 28, 1915.

In the event that one of his designs were accepted, MacNeil would be paid $2,000. If, however, his designs were rejected, he would be compensated the meager sum of $300. [2]

MacNeil expressed displeasure over the proposed $300 compensation in a letter to Woolley on Jan. 4, 1916. In this same letter, he asked for a clarification of the department's April 15 deadline for design submission and the design requirements in regard to his treatment of the representation of Liberty. [3]

MacNeil also acknowledged that he had visited the Mint during the previous week, where he discussed coinage requirements with Mint engraver Barber and George Morgan.

MacNeil officially accepted the Treasury's commission in a letter dated Jan. 11, 1916.

In a subsequent letter, he told Woolley that the three sculptors had agreed to have preliminary designs ready for submission by mid-February. He said he expected all three artists would submit their material to arrive in Washington on Feb. 21.

This timetable must have been adhered to, because on Feb. 28 Woolley notified MacNeil (informally) that the Treasury Department had accepted one of MacNeil's models for the quarter's obverse. In other words, the letter explained, MacNeil had been awarded "one-half design out of a possible three designs." [4]

The official notification came on May 23, 1916.

Two weeks prior to the official notification, Woolley wrote to MacNeil in the third letter owned by Annis, "I thank you for your note of recent date, and beg you to say I shall be in New York on Wednes-

DIRECTOR OF THE MINT

WASHINGTON

May 23, 1916.

Mr. Hermon A. MacNeil,
    Northern Boulevard,
      College Point,
        New York.

Dear Mr. MacNeil:

    It gives me pleasure to notify you formally that the designs submitted by you for the proposed new Quarter Dollar have been accepted, and are hereby approved.

Very truly yours,

[signature]

Director of the Mint.

Approved:

[signature]

Secretary.

The Treasury Department's official notification to Hermon MacNeil of the acceptance of his designs for the quarter dollar.

day, when I would like to talk to you about data for a description of the coin."

Apparently, even though formal notification had not yet been sent to the artist, the department was already working on the official written description of the design elements on MacNeil's quarter.

This was, perhaps, for inclusion in the Mint director's report of July 15, 1916, which was the first official description of the design.

Woolley wrote the following of the quarter:

> "The design of the 25-cent piece is intended to typify in a measure the awakening interest of the country to its own protection. . . . In the new design Liberty is shown as a full-length figure, front view, with head turned toward the left, stepping forward to the gateway of the country, and on the wall are inscribed the words 'In God We Trust,' which words also appear on the new half dollar, mentioned above. The left arm of the figure of Liberty is upraised, bearing the shield in the attitude of protection, from which the covering is being drawn. The right hand bears the olive branch of peace. On the field above the head is inscribed the word 'Liberty,' and on the step under her feet '1916.' The reverse of this coin necessitates by law a representation of the American eagle, and is here shown in full flight, with wings extended, sweeping across the coin." [5]

Lead impressions from the die for the quarter were submitted to Mint Director F.J.H. von Engelken by Superintendent A.M. Joyce on Oct. 13, 1916, with silver impressions following shortly thereafter.

MacNeil complains

On Jan. 11, 1917, shortly after the coins entered circulation, Mac-Neil wrote to von Engelken complaining that the coins as issued had "a resemblance to" a design he made the prior spring, one that he later "changed and modified considerably" with approval of the Mint director and the Treasury secretary. He was therefore surprised to see this discarded early modeling on the quarter in circulation. [6]

It is chronologically important to remember that even though 52,000 1916-dated coins were minted, none of these coins reached circulation until late 1916 or early 1917.

Although the Mint had hoped to have the new coins in circulation by July 1916, it ran into problems with production of the new dies, causing it to delay issue and work nights striking coins of the old design in order to meet the demands of commerce. [7]

The January 1917 issue of *The Numismatist*, likely sent to subscribers in December 1916, reports on the design for the new quarter, but admits that at press time none of the new subsidiary coins had been placed into circulation. An article by Henry Hettger and Susan Novac in the July/August 1994 issue of Bowers and Merena's *Rare Coin Review* quotes the Jan. 17, 1917, issue of the Philadelphia *Public Ledger* as recording that "the new silver quarter is at hand and in circulation."

It is, therefore, likely that MacNeil's Jan. 11, 1917, letter of complaint to von Engelken represents the artist's first glimpse of the finished product — the 1916 Type I quarter bearing a design similar to one he discarded the prior spring!

MacNeil said that after receiving the coins, he went directly to the Mint, where he "was still more surprised and interested to see the many variations that had already been on this coin, many of them arrangements that I myself had already tried and discarded." [8]

He told von Engelken that in the interest of producing the best possible design, certain modifications were needed.

For the obverse, MacNeil suggested moving Liberty's head away from the rim, preventing the figure from becoming bowlegged, and minimizing the sagging of the shield by having it pulled tighter.

For the reverse, MacNeil said the eagle had been dropped too low, which made it look (when soiled) as if the tail was connected with the lettering below. He said this gave the appearance of a low-flying or just-rising eagle, and that from his study of the bird, the talons are only extended behind when the eagle is well under way at high altitude.

He suggested that the Mint may have lowered the eagle to prevent its right wing from touching the "A" in "America" — a feature he liked and one that would reappear on the modified 1917 design. [9]

(Facing page)
Written on Jan. 11, 1917, the same day MacNeil complained to the Treasury Department about the design of the quarter, this letter confirms that MacNeil planned on "making a stand for improvements." **Courtesy of Auctions by Bowers and Merena.**

HERMON A. MAC NEIL
COLLEGE POINT
NEW YORK

Jan. 31 '17

Dear Walter

If peradventure you
should be tempted
to make any publicity
of the little quarter —
It might be well to
wait a bit as they
are not issued yet
& I am making a
stand for improvements
As I told you they have
garbled my design
yrs in haste

Herman —

85

The primary change to the quarter's reverse involved raising the eagle. MacNeil had complained that it been dropped too low, making it look (when soiled) as if the tail was connected with the lettering. He believed the Mint may have lowered the eagle to prevent the tip of the eagle's right wing from touching the "A" in "America," a feature he liked. The revised version also placed three stars just below the eagle.

The text of von Engelken's Jan. 13 reply can be found in Don Taxay's *The U.S. Mint and Coinage: An Illustrated History From 1776 to the Present*. The director informed MacNeil that "as the coins have gone into circulation, no marked changes could be undertaken." [10]

Von Engelken cautioned that "no radical changes would be considered," and that he reserved the right not to have new dies made should the new model depart from the accepted design.

Changes were made, however, incorporating not only the features called for in MacNeil's Jan. 11 letter, but to the figure of Liberty as well.

A reason for the change

An interesting handwritten letter from MacNeil to von Engelken may provide the link to the remodeling of Liberty's garments.

The letter, received by the Treasury Department on Jan. 26, 1917, reveals that after the meeting with Superintendent Joyce it was agreed that the Mint would keep the design much the same as issued, "merely substituting the second modeling of the figure for the present one." [11]

MacNeil said this would give practically the same figure, but it would be "more resonant and purposeful & solidly constructed — very much like the difference between a good egg & bad egg superficially about same — but when you look into it, very different." [12]

The "second modeling" was likely the chain-mail version of Liberty that appeared in mid-1917. Though the Treasury Department made no "official" mention of this aspect in approving the design changes, without any form of public outcry against the first version, there wouldn't have been any reason for comment.

In a notice datelined from Washington Feb. 6, 1917, it was announced that the Mint was considering slight changes to the design at MacNeil's request, noting that:

> "Treasury officials are considering the matter on the suggestion of the designer of the coins Herman McNeill [sic] of New York. McNeill [sic] is said to have suggested placing on the obverse [sic, reverse] side of the coin a background of stars against the figure of the eagle and slightly raising the design of the eagle." [13]

In an April 16, 1917, letter to Rep. William Ashbrook, chairman of the House Committee on Coinage, Weights, and Measures, McAdoo said similarly (in reference to an act to modify the design) that the

The most noticeable modification to the obverse was the addition of a chain-mail covering over Liberty's upper torso.

modifications proposed were considered "slight."

The changes included, according to McAdoo, the raising of the eagle on the reverse, the addition of three stars beneath the eagle, rearrangement of the lettering, and the addition of a slight concavity to the surface.

McAdoo concluded, "I am sorry to have to ask for this change, but since the original dies were made the artist has found that they are not true to the original design and that a great improvement can be made in the artistic value and appearance of the coin by making the slight changes the act contemplates." [14]

The act (H.R. 3548), approved July 9, 1917, is reprinted in the Mint director's report for 1917 and confirms that the changes were of an artistic nature and were to be in place by July 1, 1918.

MacNeil apparently found all of the changes acceptable. In an Aug. 13, 1917, letter, he wrote to Mint Director R.S. Baber, "I am much pleased to get your announcement that the Quarter Dollar is lawfully back to an artistic basis and is now being minted." [15]

As an interesting side note to MacNeil's concern over the Mint's alterations to his design (as it appeared on the 1916 and 1917 Type I coins), in 1988 Bowers and Merena Inc. of Wolfeboro, N.H., auctioned a presentation frame containing a 1916 Standing Liberty quarter and a handwritten letter from MacNeil written on the same date (Jan. 11, 1917) as his letter of complaint to von Engelken about the Mint's substitution of designs.

The frame was included in Bowers and Merena's sale of the Lloyd M. Higgins, M.D., Collection, held Jan. 28-30, 1988, in Los Angeles.

The letter, presented with the quarter, is addressed to a Walter M. Pratt of Boston. It states:

> "If per adventure you should be tempted to make any publicity of the little quarter — it might be well to wait a bit as they are not issued yet & I am making a stand for improvements. As I told you they have garbled my design." [16]

Protest lacking

Besides the written comments of MacNeil, the tone of the comments by the editor and letters found in *The Numismatist* would tend to belie any belief that the changes were made on the basis of public outrage over nudity depicted on the coin. In fact, the coin's obverse was described in the January 1917 issue as being "strikingly beautiful."

Likewise, letters to the editor made no complaint about the nudi-

In 1925 the design of the Standing Liberty quarter was again altered, this time to place the date in recess to protect it from wear.

ty, noting only that the obverse could be termed "stately," "beautiful and artistic," "perfect in every detail," the small amount of criticism being leveled at the eagle on the coin's reverse as not being ornithologically correct. [17]

The March 1917 issue of *The Numismatist* gave the first inkling of a redesign, saying that press dispatches from Washington contained information that change was being contemplated. MacNeil, it said, had suggested placing a background of stars around the eagle and slightly raising its design. [18]

Even when the announcement of the design change was made in the August 1917 issue, no mention was made of any form of public protest against the Type I coin, only that a press dispatch from Washington claimed that the coin was found to accumulate dirt too easily, and that the Mint had begun work on new dies. [19]

The primary design changes were made to the reverse, said Farran Zerbe, with the eagle placed higher, and a new arrangement of stars. Of the obverse, he said, "the features of the head of Liberty are stronger. The sprig in her hand does not engage the 'L.' There are fewer dots in the shield, and the undraped chaste bust of the old has been given what looks like a corsage of mail.' " [20]

Under the heading "Miss Liberty Now in a Gown Mail?" the editorial in the same issue of *The Numismatist* did question the intention of the designer in placing Liberty in the new covering, wondering if had anything to do with country's movement from a state of "preparedness" displayed on the initial design to one reflecting its subsequent entry into World War I. [21]

If there was significant public protest to the nudity on the Type I design, it was well hidden. *The Numismatist* and its readers were never beyond making clear exactly how they felt about a coinage design. Nor has the public ever been.

Beyond artistic considerations, the only other concern raised in House and Senate debate over the design change was the coin's inability to properly stack, a concern addressed in the redesign and likely of importance in the decision to grant the artist his concessions.

Following the alterations, MacNeil's Standing Liberty quarter continued to be minted through 1930, with one other design change in 1925. At that time, the date was lowered to protect it from wear.

MacNeil died in October 1947, more than 30 years after his quarter first entered circulation.

With his passing he left a legacy of great American sculpture, including one of the finest coins ever produced.

Chapter 6

Washington's silver

Did the first president donate the silver for the nation's first coins?

OK. So George Washington didn't chop down a cherry tree or throw a silver dollar across the Potomac, but was his silverware really used to create the nation's first coinage?

Well, it's kind of hard to say for certain either way. It's one of the most cherished stories in all of U.S. coin history, one of the oldest, and one that even if it should someday be proven false, would likely continue to be clung to with religious reverence by collectors.

For those unfamiliar with this romantic tale, tradition tells that President George Washington was so anxious to begin coinage that the nation's first coins were struck even prior to the purchase of a site for the new mint — coinage beginning on a small screw press housed in a Philadelphia building owned by John Harper.

Thus, at the time the now-famous 1792 half dismes were struck, the new Mint had no buildings, no land, no depositors and, above all, no silver for coinage. The metal had to come from somewhere and that somewhere, the story goes, was silverware provided by George and Martha Washington. This, then, was stamped into the half dimes Washington referred to during his fourth annual address to Congress as a "small beginning" to the nation's coinage.

Likely, 1,500 were struck, with estimates of the survival of these wafer-thin half dimes placing the number still extant at less than 100. Today, even heavily worn examples draw the attention of col-

The traditional story is that the 1792 half disme, of which less than 100 are believed to exist today, was minted from silver donated by George and Martha Washington.

lectors when put up for sale, not only because the coins are rare but because of the personal link to Washington and his reshaped eating utensils.

Vintage tale

The story of Washington's silver is a vintage one, first told in the classic 19th century tomes on U.S. coinage. Sylvester Sage Crosby, for example, recorded in his 1875 work, *The Early Coins of America*, that "tradition reports, that, owing to the scarcity of silver, Washington caused some of his own private plate to be melted to supply the deficiency, and that it was from that supply that these patterns were coined." [1]

Likewise, Frank H. Stewart, in his *History of the United States Mint and Its Operations*, commented:

> "It has been claimed, and it is probably true, that the half 'dismes' he [Washington] mentioned in his fourth annual address to Congress were made from silver furnished by him. They are even today known as Washington half dimes." [2]

A likely source

Beyond the scattered references to "Washington half dimes" found in 19th century numismatic accounts of U.S. coinage, the pri-

Another popular legend concerning the 1792 half disme is that the obverse was modeled after Martha Washington. It's a story pretty much dismissed today. **Painting by Charles Willson Peale. Courtesy Independence National Historical Park.**

Painting by John Ward Dunsmore titled Inspection of the First Coins of the First United States Mint (ca. 1916), commissioned by Frank Stewart. Chief Coiner Henry Voigt (right front) is shown with a tray of the new half dismes. Mint Director David Rittenhouse stands next to Martha Washington, with George Washington behind her. Adam Eckfeldt is shown operating a screw press at right.

mary source of evidence cited today as confirmation that Washington donated his private silver for the coinage, used the new coins as gifts, and caused $100 worth (2,000) of the new half dimes to be struck, is an April 9, 1844, memorandum from Jonas R. McClintock, a Mint melter and refiner, said to have been a close friend of Adam Eckfeldt.

Eckfeldt's lengthy association with the Mint began with the 1792 coinage and continued into the 1850s. The Eckfeldt family, and presumably Adam Eckfeldt, were also apparently the source of many of the stories or "traditions" about Washington's interest in the first mint. [3]

The McClintock memorandum, which began with a description of the obverse and reverse of the 1792 half disme, reads:

> "In conversation with Mr. Adam Eckfeldt today at the mint, he informed me that the Half Dismes above described were struck at the request of Gen. Washington to the extent of one hundred dollars which sum he deposited in bullion or specie — for that purpose — Mr. Eckfeldt thinks that Gen. Washington distributed them as presents — some were sent to Europe but the greater number of them he believes, were given to acquaintances in Virginia. No more of them were coined except those for Gen. Washington. They were never designed as currency — the mint was not at the time fully ready for going into operation. The coining machinery was in the cellar of Mr. Harper's sawmaker at the corner of Cherry and Sixth Streets, at which place these pieces were struck." [4]

The contents of the memorandum, with minor variations from above, also appear in Don Taxay's *The U.S. Mint and Coinage: An Illustrated History From 1776 to the Present.* Taxay said the original memorandum was owned by Walter Breen and was shown publicly for the first time in the April 20, 1960, issue of *Coin World.* He adds that the memorandum was discovered by Edward B. Haden and published in the May 1943 issue of *The Numismatist;* correct identification of the letter's author, McClintock, coming from reader Charles McSorley in the July 1943 issue of the same journal. [5]

It may surprise some, therefore, that this "memorandum" was in reality a piece of paper pasted to the flyleaf of a used book on foreign coins, found by Haden at Leary's Book Store in Philadelphia. What's more surprising, and a bit distressing, is that the piece of paper was signed only as "J Mc" or, as first reported, "I McAllister," but has since come to be positively identified as representing "Jonas R. McClintock," rising in some accounts from an official-sounding "memorandum" to the status of an even more official-sounding "document."

One can certainly assume that the bookstore's location, Philadelphia, would lend more readily to validity of the attribution to McClintock. It can also be assumed that few, if any, would have had likely cause to make up such a story and go through the trouble of pasting it in this and, according to McSorley, several other books found in the same store. Yet these would only be assumptions, correct or incorrect.

The memorandum was, as Taxay wrote, first published in the May 1943 issue of *The Numismatist*. Haden explained in his letter to the editor that it was signed "I McAllister." According to McSorley, Haden's attribution to an "I McAllister" was based on a penciled-in notation by someone apparently attempting to identify the memorandum's author from a mistaken interpretation of the initials. The memorandum, he said, was "signed in faded, hardly legible brown ink" as "J Mc," who he identified as McClintock, Eckfeldt's friend. McClintock is listed in George Evans' *Illustrated History of the United States Mint* as having been employed by the Mint as an officer and a refiner. [6]

Serious questions

Even if we assume the memorandum is genuine and derived from McClintock's hand, inconsistencies in it contents, as to the intended use of these coins and the number struck, raise some serious questions.

The memorandum implies that the 1792 half dismes deserve no greater status than patterns for a proposed coinage, or worse, as medals, issued at the whim of the president to be given away casually as fanciful little gifts to acquaintances in Philadelphia and Europe.

According to the memorandum, the coins were never intended as currency. If this is true, then Washington's address to Congress, in which he made reference to the "small beginning" of the coinage of half dimes, explaining that "the want of small coin in circulation calling first attention to them," was either in error or an outright attempt by Washington to mislead Congress. More likely, his statement to Congress denoted his wishes that these first federally-issued coins circulate and be accepted as coins of the realm.

The need for a sound circulating coinage was dearly felt. Washington once charged that "a man must travel with a pair of scales in his pocket, or run the risk of receiving gold at one-forth less than it counts." Some of the new coins may have been presented by Washington as gifts, but the majority would likely have been placed into circulation as originally intended.

Researcher Andrew Pollock has also questioned the inconsistencies in the McClintock memorandum. In his 1994 book, *United States Patterns and Related Issues*, Pollock said that if we are to believe that the first half dimes were truly intended as gifts, then most recipients didn't keep their gifts, as much of the surviving coinage has "seen extensive circulation." [7]

There is also some discrepancy in the memorandum's account of the number of examples struck. This difference has led many to quote the mintage of 1792 half dismes as falling between 1,500 and 2,000.

The most credible reference to the number of these coins minted was discovered by Taxay in the papers of Thomas Jefferson held by the Library of Congress. According to Taxay, on July 13, 1792, Jefferson, who was then charged with oversight of Mint matters, recorded the delivery of 1,500 half dismes. [8]

However, Breen recorded in the March-April 1954 issue of *The Coin Collector's Journal* that additional confirmation for the traditional figure of 2,000 can be found in a book held by the National Archives, titled *Coinage and Expenses 1792-1835*. Interestingly, he attributes the likely source for this number to Eckfeldt, the supposed basis for the same figure found in the McClintock memorandum. [9]

In conclusion, Breen properly warns that a "tradition" can lead to the formation of today's "hypothesis" and, thereafter, become tomorrow's "fact." It's an observation that is seemingly justified in this instance. For it's likely that the source for the "tradition" that Washington provided silver for the nation's first coinage, that 2,000 coins pieces were struck, and that the coins were intended as gifts, originated with Eckfeldt's memory of the operations of the first mint.

This doesn't mean that he was wrong, but consideration must be given to the fact that by the time of the McClintock memorandum Eckfeldt was 75 years old. In light of the inconsistencies between his memories and contemporary sources, the suggestion is strong that his account of events that happened 50 years earlier is more likely askew than the 18th century comments of Washington and Jefferson.

Could Washington have supplied silver for the first coinage? Yes. Considering the Mint's early problems with obtaining metal for coinage, it may even be likely. It's just another one of those stories where, unfortunately, a well-traveled tale remains the only, somewhat potholed, source of verification.

Chapter 7

A pretend Indian?

Of Indians, a young girl, family lore, and the Indian Head cent

Cents have always been popular with collectors. This is especially true of the Indian Head cent, struck for circulation from 1859-1909.

For history buffs, it evokes images of the Old West via its Liberty adorned with an Indian headdress. For others, it is a reminder of a cheerful tale of a young girl, an Indian chief and a loving father who placed her likeness on a U.S. coin for all to admire.

Alas, though, like so many other "twisted tails," it's a story entrenched primarily in numismatic lore.

A bit of malarkey

"It was a bright, sunny morning in 1835 when a group of Indians, who had been in Washington, D.C., to visit the Great White Chief, stopped by the U.S. Mint in Philadelphia. Their visit came just as James B. Longacre (Mint chief engraver 1828-1840) was showing his 12-year-old daughter, Sarah, the workings of the Mint.

"An old chief, attracted by the sweet-faced maiden who had taken an interest in his Indian headdress, placed the warbonnet on the young girl's head. It was such a striking picture that Longacre immediately took up sketch pad and began to draw his daughter in her borrowed headgear.

One of the most popular of all numismatic tales is that the obverse of James B. Longacre's Indian Head cent (1859-1909) was modeled after his daughter during a visit of Native Americans to Washington, D.C. According to this tradition, young Sarah Longacre modeled one of the Indian's headdresses, which inspired her father to make the drawing of her later employed on the cent. It's a story disputed by many but with a long tradition among Longacre descendants.

"The proud father, having previously entered a design competition for the new cent, and having racked his brain for an original and singular design with which to impress the judges, thought to himself that perhaps the combination of the Indian headfeathers and Saxon sweetness could win the prize.

"He submitted the drawing, surviving through several rounds of competition to finally have his design selected, winning the competition by one vote over more than 1,000 entries. Thus, his young daughter came to be immortalized on the nation's humblest of coins."

This bit of malarkey isn't quoted directly from anywhere, though it is a condensed version of a nonsensical story that appeared in a major numismatic publication quite some time ago. It can't be certain where the author got his penchant for spicing his story with liberal doses of pure imagination, though he claimed to be quoting directly from a Longacre relative. If he was, well, there's this bridge in Brooklyn, you see, and it's real, real cheap.

First, there was no competition for the design of the Indian Head cent. Mint chief engraver James B. Longacre designed it, plain and simple. Second, the coin wasn't released until 1859, 24 years after this story takes place. Third, Longacre's term at the Mint wasn't 1828-1840, rather 1844-1869.

Yet even within this fanciful tale there lies a bit of the problem that seemingly plagues numismatists at every turn — a "good story" has become so intermixed with the facts that it's hard to tell what's true anymore.

Relative memories

Even though the account above is seething with flaws, it was not the only instance in which a Longacre relative told of a visit by Native Americans to James B. Longacre's home or the U.S. Mint (generally between 1844 and 1849), where young Sarah Longacre (most often age 12, sometimes 6, sometimes 16), posed for her father in Indian headdress, inspiring his design for the Indian Head cent.

One of those versions was provided in the November 1931 issue of *The Numismatist*. It quoted a press dispatch from Falls City, Neb., saying:

"Add to your list of famous 'debunkers' Mrs. Sarah Peck, ninety-one-year-old resident of this city. For those Americans who believe the feather bedecked head which appears on the Indian penny is that of some Indian, Mrs.

Peck has this information:

"The 'chief' was not an Indian at all. The picture is that of a little white girl, Mrs. Sarah Longacre Keen, a distant relative of Mrs. Peck.

"As a girl of 12 Mrs. Keen visited her father at the United States Mint at Philadelphia, where he was employed as chief engraver. A competition was on for sketches for the design of the new copper cent.

"A number of Indians, with their chief, visited the mint. The chief let the little girl wear his headgear. The effect was so striking that the father made a sketch, submitted it in the competition and won the award." [1]

Casting aspersions

Those who cast aspersions on this old family tale will tell you that the Indian Head cent's design is largely a repeat of that appearing on the gold dollar beginning in 1849, the double eagle of the same year, and later employed, in 1854, on the gold $3 piece. They'll also tell you correctly that Longacre once denied having used his daughter as a model.

One of the first to question the tale's validity was Mint chief engraver Charles Barber. In an article for *Sunset Magazine*, published shortly after coinage of the Indian Head cent had ended, Barber observed that it was hard to disprove a story of this kind. Most people, he said, "do not want any evidence to upset a pretty romance such as is now woven around this coin, any more than they are anxious for fact that will cast doubt upon the origin of our flag and the Betsy Ross romance." [2]

Barber added that although it was impossible at that late date (1910) to prove what Longacre used as a model, there was sufficient evidence "to satisfy an unprejudiced mind that he did not use either his daughter or an Indian war bonnet." [3]

Barber's source in this determination was a Mint employee, who, he said, remembered distinctly Longacre's sentiments regarding portraits on coins and that the engraver would have opposed using his daughter. The Mint employee, Barber said, also remembered that it was Longacre's aim to portray an "ideal head" of an Indian female.

More striking, Barber claimed, is that the features of Liberty on the 1849 double eagle are the same as the cent.

It has been argued by those who dispute the story of Sarah Long-acre's modeling for her father's coin that the depiction of Liberty on the cent is the same as the classical Liberty he created for the earlier gold dollar, gold double eagle and gold $3 coin.

"Now, if the child was only six years old in 1859 when the cent was executed, she certainly was not used for the model head in 1849," he wrote. [4] It was inconceivable to Barber that anyone looking at the Liberty on the cent could believe the features were those of a six-year-old girl or even a young girl. [5]

The same basic head, Barber said, is found on the $3 gold coin and on a pattern coin with a seated figure. He complained that it was apparently incomprehensible to most people that an artist working on the design of a head or face "has not the most remote idea of making a portrait," even though he may have used a model. Barber added:

> "We have heard it said many times, all of which is untrue, that the Longacre head upon the double eagle was his wife's, that the head upon the standard dollar is that of a Philadelphia school teacher, that the head upon the rare eagle is a portrait of an Irish girl in the employ of Mr. Saint-Gaudens. Although, Homer Saint-Gaudens, the artist's son, tells us the latter was a study for the Victory of the Sherman statue." [6]

As for the Indian headdress, Barber said the feathers in the cent's design are not those of a warbonnet and could not have been sketched from any real bonnet taken from any head of any Indian.

Numismatic scholar Walter Breen also questioned the story behind Sarah Longacre's posing for the Indian Head cent.

In the April 1951 issue of *Numismatic Scrapbook Magazine* Breen wrote that the debate could be laid to rest by the records of the National Archives.

According to Breen, Longacre planned to apply the head designed for the gold dollar in 1849 to other denominations, except the double eagle. Of the double eagle, Longacre wrote in a letter to the Treasury secretary, "The entire design, arrangement and execution are my own — the artistic proportions of the head are from antique, and will be found to correspond very nearly with those of the **Venus Acroupii**, a favorite standard." [7]

Breen determined that in no way was Longacre portraying any individual, rather a Hellenic pattern, the same as he did for the $3 gold piece.

Breen also quotes a Nov. 4, 1858, letter from Mint Director James Ross Snowden to Treasury Secretary Howell Cobb in which Snowden says the obverse shows "an ideal head of America — the drooping plumes of the North American Indian giving it the character of North America." [8]

In conclusion, Breen wrote, "in no case was anything but an ideal head of Liberty" intended. The coin was based "squarely on the classical profiles on ancient sculpture."

In a 1968 article for *Coins* magazine Breen said similarly:

> "Suffice it to say that the head [on the $3 gold coin] does not depict any Indian, but rather (even as with the other gold) a Greco-Roman statue, probably the same Venus Accroupie which Longacre used ever since 1849. The three drawings reproduced here, as presented in [Don] Taxay's previously mentioned work, plainly prove that one and the same engraving of a statue — and no Indian, nor yet Sarah Longacre, who was not even out of swaddling clothes in 1849 when Longacre first created this profile — served as the source for the Liberty heads Longacre put on gold and the 'Indian' head he put on the cent." [9]

Relative questions

Even with the detractors, and a denial by Longacre, the stories continued, largely propagated by Longacre's descendents, who insisted that the basis of the tale was true, even if the particulars were a bit messed up.

For example, grandson Rev. Lindsay B. Longacre took exception to the Breen article, writing in the November 1951 issue of *Numismatic Scrapbook Magazine* that although it was not impossible that the story behind the visit of the Indians was fabricated, it could also have been based on fact. [10]

Lindsay Longacre wrote that from childhood he knew James Longacre's daughter, Sarah, as his Aunt Sallie. His father often told him the story of a "commission of Indians" who came to Washington on government business. Two of them visited with his grandfather at Longacre's home in Philadelphia. They laid aside their headdresses and Sallie picked one up, putting it on her head. Longacre then sketched her.

Lindsay Longacre maintained that the coin was idealized from this sketch. This story, he said, did not preclude the use of a classical ideal, as Breen had argued, nor did it necessitate an actual portrait.

Additional support

Additional support for the Longacre family story came from Joy Goforth in an article in the Jan. 4, 1984, issue of *Coin World*, reprinted from the November 1983 issue of *Mint Press*, a publication of the U.S. Mint. [11]

Goforth said that genealogy provided by the Longacre family shows Sarah Longacre would have been in range of 16 to 21 years of age during the period of 1844-1849, making the tale of her posing more likely, as she would have advanced beyond childhood.

In answer to Barber's reference to Sarah as being six years old, she recorded that Sarah's younger sister, Eliza Huldah Longacre, was born in May 1837 and would have been only 7 to 12 years of age in 1844 (or six if the visit came before her birthday). Mint workers, she said, may have confused Eliza for Sarah.

Cent specialist Rick Snow also finds support for the theory that Sarah Longacre may have served as the inspiration for her father's coinage designs, although he puts a different twist on the story.

In his 1994 work, *Flying Eagle and Indian Cents*, Snow said a sepia of Sarah Longacre by her father, circa 1840, compares favorably to the design on the coin.

According to Snow, the sepia matches a later sketch of Sarah Longacre found in Longacre's sketchbook. The same sketchbook, Snow said, also contains Longacre's "other small cent sketches, including the Indian Cent prototype sketches." [12] Snow wrote:

"The most noticeable feature is the 'Longacre nose' whose profile lines run straight from the tip to the forehead. The eyebrows, lips, and chin shape are very similar on all these sketches." [13]

He also contends that the Indian Head cent's depiction was not based on the design for the $20 gold piece and the $3 piece, but bears different features from those coins. The $20 and $3 coins, he said, may indeed

The sepia drawing of Sarah Longacre. Courtesy of the National Portrait Gallery.

have been modeled after the Italian statue *Venus Acroupie* ("Crouching Venus"), as Breen suggested. The cent, he said, was not.

Snow conceded that there is no solid proof, just the suggestion that this sketch may have served as the basis for the coin. He added that the story may never be proven satisfactorily either way.

He is probably right. The tale of Native Americans and a young girl has made colorful copy for writers for years and will most likely continue to do so. For as tales go, this one brings with it unquestionable allure.

Chapter 8

A perfect model

Research by a relative of black model Hettie Anderson leads to a likely model for the Saint-Gaudens $20 gold coin

If you've been a collector for some time you've probably heard that an Irish lass, Mary Cunningham, served as the model for Augustus Saint-Gaudens' graceful, striding figure of Liberty on the gold double eagle, released in 1907. Failing that, you've been told that Alice Butler modeled for the coin. Or, that Saint-Gaudens' mistress, Davida Clark, should be so honored.

You've probably never heard of Hettie Anderson. Or, maybe you have, only in a rather vague and often overlooked reference. She's the "woman supposed to have negro blood in her veins" once referred to by the artist's son, Homer Saint-Gaudens, as a possible model.

It probably wouldn't have sat too well with the blue bloods of Homer Saint-Gaudens' day if they found out that a black woman served as a model for the nation's $20 gold coin. However, it now appears that the Saint-Gaudens double eagle may indeed have been modeled after Hettie Anderson, an African-American woman from New York.

This discovery was made in 1991 by William E. Hagans, a relative of Anderson's, and was first published in Krause Publications' weekly

High-relief examples of the 1907 Saint-Gaudens double eagle are among the most stunning of all U.S. coins. It took several blows from the coining press to bring the design up fully, something Mint officials deemed impractical for the purposes of a modern, high-speed coinage facility.

newspaper for coin collectors, *Numismatic News*. It startled some then, and it will likely do so now.

Saint-Gaudens, the artist

To learn the story of Anderson and her modeling for Saint-Gaudens is to learn of an artist who fervently believed, as did President Theodore Roosevelt, that the nation's coinage should be raised to a loftier artistic standard — similar to the impressive high-relief, hand-struck coins of ancient Greece.

By his own account, published as *The Reminiscences of Augustus Saint-Gaudens*, Saint-Gaudens was born on March 1, 1848, in Dublin, Ireland, to Bernard and Mary (McGuiness) Saint-Gaudens.

His family emigrated to America shortly after his birth. Arriving in late 1848, they settled in New York, where his father was engaged in manufacturing shoes.

In 1861, Saint-Gaudens, then 13, began the formal pursuit of a career in art, finding work producing cameos as an apprentice for New York stone cameo-cutter Louis Avet during the day (a period described by Saint-Gaudens as years "of miserable slavery") and taking art classes at the Cooper Institute at night.

Leaving Avet, in 1864, Saint-Gaudens took employment with another stone cutter, Jules Le Brethen, a shell cameo-cutter for whom he worked for the following three years while engaging additional art studies at the National Academy of Design.

In 1867, with passage paid by his father, Saint-Gaudens set out on the first of several extended stays in Europe. In Paris, while awaiting acceptance to the prestigious Ecole des Beaux-Arts, he took a position cutting cameos for a jeweler by the name of Lupi and studied at Ecole gratuite de Dessin, where he modeled his first figure in the nude.

The following year he was admitted to the Ecole des Beaux-Arts, joining the atelier of Francois Jouffroy, an artist best noted for his sculpture *The Secret of Venus*, the figure of a young girl whispering into the ear of Hermes.

With the outbreak of the Franco-Prussian War, Saint-Gaudens moved to Rome and took a studio with another artist and began his marble sculpture, *Hiawatha*, the legendary Iroquois Nation chief.

In 1872 he returned to the United States, working in a studio in New York, where one of his commissions (for the Masonic Temple in New York) was *Silence*, the marble figure of cloaked woman gesturing for silence.

Augustus Saint-Gaudens made his entry into the world of coinage design late in his career. By the 1900s he was already established as one of the nation's pre-eminent sculptors. Photograph by D.C. Ward.

Saint-Gaudens' first major commission came in the late 1870s, when he sculpted a monument to Navy Adm. David Farragut for Madison Square in New York City.

He again went abroad the following year, where he met Augusta Homer of Boston, whom he would eventually marry. His stay this time was brief. Low on funds, he returned to New York in 1875 and set up a studio.

It was during this period that he received one of his first major commissions, a bronze statue of Civil War Navy Adm. David Farragut for Madison Square Park in New York. Two years later he married Augusta, helped found the Society of American Artists, and again set off for Europe, not returning to the United States until 1880.

His reputation as a master sculptor continued to grow, as did his list of commissions. Notable in a brief listing of his most memorable monuments are the *Shaw Memorial*, Boston Common, Boston; the *Puritan*, Fairmount Park, Philadelphia; *General John A. Logan Monument*, Grant Park, Chicago; *Roswell P. Flower Monument*, Watertown, N.Y.; *Adams Memorial*, Rock Creek Church Cemetery, Washington, D.C.; *Diana*, Philadelphia Museum of Art; and two figures of Lincoln

— *Abraham Lincoln: The Head of State* (seated), Grant Park, and *Abraham Lincoln: The Man* (seated), Lincoln Park, both in Chicago.

In 1892 he received a commission to prepare a monument in honor of Civil War Gen. William T. Sherman for the Grand Army Plaza in New York, work on which was begun in New York, continued upon his return to Paris in 1897, and completed in the United States. [1]

In 1900 he won the Grand Prize at the Paris Exposition. Featured among his exhibits were the *General Sherman* and *Victory* of the *Sherman Monument.*

Saint-Gaudens returned to the United States in 1900, setting up a studio in Cornish, N.H.

During his long career he had many assistants and students, several of whom are very familiar to coin collectors, including Adolph Weinman (Mercury dime and Walking Liberty half dollar), James Earle Fraser (Indian Head nickel, Oregon Trail half dollar), Hermon MacNeil (Standing Liberty quarter), John Flanagan (Washington quarter) and Bela Lyon Pratt (Indian Head $2.50 and $5 gold).

A 'pet crime'

It was over a dinner in Washington, D.C., in the winter of 1905, that Roosevelt and Saint-Gaudens began to discuss the possibility of redesigning the nation's gold coinage. Roosevelt first became acquainted with Saint-Gaudens through the latter's appointment as a consultant to the Board of Public Buildings, working to implement the McMillan Plan (an effort to make civic improvements in the District of Columbia), and through Saint-Gaudens' labors in Washington to establish an American Academy in Rome. [2] Saint-Gaudens also designed Roosevelt's inaugural medal, the modeling for which was done by his assistant, Weinman.

Throughout the period of their acquaintance, up until Saint-Gaudens' death from cancer in 1907, the artist and the president were in regular correspondence, generally in relation to Roosevelt's "pet crime," the redesign of the nation's coinage. Thanks to the efforts of Homer Saint-Gaudens, the text of these letters have been preserved and published, showing the channels by which the $10 and $20 gold coins were remodeled in 1907.

The content of the letters has been transcribed in many numismatic sources since, but initially appeared in the April 1920 publication of "Roosevelt and Our Coin Designs: Letters Between Theodore Roosevelt and Augustus Saint-Gaudens" by *Century Illustrated Monthly Magazine.*

In a Nov. 6, 1905, letter to Saint-Gaudens, President Theodore Roosevelt expressed his desire to have a high-relief coinage similar to the ancient Greek gold coins of Alexander the Great.

On Nov. 6, 1905, Roosevelt wrote to Saint-Gaudens requesting that the artist provide an update as to what progress had been made, asking, "How is that old gold coinage design getting along?"

Roosevelt suggested that it seemed worthwhile "to try for a really good coinage, though I suppose there will be a revolt about it!" Roosevelt's reference to a "good coinage" reflecting his admiration for the coins of ancient Greece.

"I was looking at some gold coins of Alexander the Great today, and I was struck by their high relief," he wrote to Saint-Gaudens. "Would it not be well to have our coins in high relief, and also to have the rims raised?" The raising of the rims, he said, would protect the high-relief design from wear. [3]

Saint-Gaudens responded on Nov. 11, 1905:

> "You have hit the nail on the head with regard to the coinage. Of course the great coins (and you might almost say the only coins) are the Greek ones you speak of, just as the great medals are those of the fifteenth century by Pisanello and Sperandio." [4]

Saint-Gaudens said he would be pleased to undertake a redesign, but feared Mint officials would "throw fits" because of the problems with striking coins in high relief, namely the number of blows necessary to bring up the design and the inability to do so and still maintain the high-speed coinage expected of a modern mint.

Saint-Gaudens was no neophyte when it came to these concerns. Having tangled with Mint chief engraver Charles Barber in relation to his inaugural medal for Roosevelt, he was rightfully reticent about approaching the Mint on his own, telling Roosevelt that he thought there could be no objection to such coins if the rims could be raised high enough to prevent rubbing, but intimating that it was perhaps better if the inquiry came from Roosevelt, so as not to incur "the antagonistic reply from those who have the say in such matters that would certainly be made to me." [5]

Admitting that he hadn't as yet prepared any models for the coins, only sketches, Saint-Gaudens told the president he anticipated placing an eagle similar to the one used for the reverse of Roosevelt inaugural medal on one side of the gold double eagle and, on the other, a figure of Liberty, possibly winged, ". . . striding energetically forward as if on a mountain top holding aloft on one arm a shield bearing the Stars and Stripes with the word Liberty marked across the field, in the other hand, perhaps, a flaming torch. The drapery would be flowing in the breeze. My idea is to make it a *living* thing and typical of progress." [6] The figure was no doubt inspired by his *Victory* for the *Sherman Monument*, which Roosevelt admired.

The artist added that he remembered Roosevelt spoke of the possible use of a head of an Indian, but wondered if it would be "a sufficiently clear emblem of Liberty" to meet the provisions of the law.

In a Nov. 14, 1905, letter to Saint-Gaudens, Roosevelt said he would summon the Mint people and try to persuade them "that coins of the Grecian type," but with raised rim, would meet the needs of commerce. He also suggested the possibility of adding an Indian feather headdress. Roosevelt wrote:

"If we get down to bed-rock facts would the feather head-dress be any more out of keeping with the rest of Liberty than the canonical Phrygian cap which never is worn and never has been worn by any free people in the world?"[7]

A little more than a week later Saint-Gaudens wrote in agreement that an Indian headdress would be appropriate. "It should be very handsome," he told the president. [8]

Early designs for the gold coinage featured the figure of Liberty with the addition of angel wings, a headdress and a shield. **Photograph by D.C. Ward.**

On Jan. 7, 1906, Saint-Gaudens wrote to Adolph Weinman in search of an Indian headdress. A little more than a month later he again queried Weinman, this time for angel wings. [9]

Whether or not either query has direct reference to the coinage design cannot be positively ascertained. Yet the suggest is strong, as it wasn't until late in May of that year that Saint-Gaudens reported to Roosevelt that the reverse of the double eagle was done and work was beginning on the obverse.

Early sketches depicted Liberty as a winged figure, with shield and feathered headdress. At one point, Saint-Gaudens contemplated adding the words "Justice" and "Liberty" to the shield.

Eventually it was decided to use a head in profile (originally planned for the cent) on the $10 gold eagle. Thus, Roosevelt was able to have his feathered headdress, which replaced an olive wreath on an earlier design. The standing eagle, first contemplated for the double eagle, was adopted for the coin's reverse.

For the reverse of the gold double eagle, a flying eagle, patterned after the obverse of James B. Longacre's Flying Eagle cent (1856-1858), was selected. This same design was originally proposed for an anticipated redesign of the cent.

Relief too high

Due to his declining health, Saint-Gaudens gave the duty of modeling over to an assistant, Henry Hering. From the start, Hering experienced problems with the Mint and, in particular, Saint-Gaudens' nemesis Charles Barber, who consistently rejected modelings as being unsuitable for high-speed modern coinage.

Hering gave a detailed vent to his feelings toward the Mint and its chief engraver in an article, "History of the $10 and $20 Gold Coins of 1907 Issue," in the August 1949 issue of *The Numismatist*.

Hering explained that due to Saint-Gaudens' ill health, he had been charged with executing the modeling of the $10 and $20 coins from Saint-Gaudens' original designs and with dealing with the Mint on a one-to-one basis.

"I proceeded to make a model in very high relief, knowing perfectly well they could not stamp it in one strike, my object being to have a die made of this model and then have strikes made in order to see the various results," Hering wrote of early work on the gold $20. [10]

He took this plaster model (measuring nearly 9 inches in diameter) to the Mint, where he was introduced to Barber. Barber rejected

A unique $20 gold pattern shows the obverse adopted for the $10 gold coin and the reverse employed on the $20 denomination. The reverse was inspired by James B. Longacre's Flying Eagle cent (1856-1858).

Plaster models for gold $20. Saint-Gaudens' assistant Henry Hering, who did the modeling of the coin from Saint-Gaudens' design sketches, found little support for the efforts of coinage redesign from officials at the U.S. Mint. Even after the installation of a Janvier lathe to improve the quality of reductions, chief engraver Charles Barber complained that the coin was not practical. Courtesy of the U.S. Department of the Interior, National Park Service, Saint-Gaudens National Historic Site, Cornish, N.H.

the model as being impossible to strike by any mint. It was only "after considerable discussion" that Barber agreed to make the die.

Hering returned to the studio and started work on a second modeling in lower relief. He was just about finished when the Mint informed him that the die of the first model was ready for experiment.

"I immediately went to Philadelphia carrying the second and revised model with me," he wrote. "When I showed it to Mr. Barber it was no more practical than the first model and he refused to have anything to do with it." [11]

The change in relief from the proposed design to the coin as issued was so dramatic that Henry Hering at first refused to give his approval to the coinage. He relented at a meeting with Mint officials in the spring of 1908.

Tests were conducted with the experimental die of the first model, Hering relating that the first stamping with 172 tons of hydraulic pressure showed "a little more than one-half the modeling." It would take until the ninth strike before the coin was brought to full detail.

"This coin I took to show to Mr. St. Gaudens, who in turn sent it to the President, and I think Mrs. Theodore Roosevelt still has it. I do not know of any more being struck, as we had finished with that die," he wrote. [12]

Hering decided to make a third model, which Barber also rejected. Ultimately, this modeling, with its relief further reduced by the Mint, would be used for the regular-issue coinage.

"Between all these events I examined the reduction of my model, which seemed to me very poor, Mr. Barber claiming it could not be done better," Hering continued. [13] Aware from his student days in Paris that a sculptor named Janvier had invented a reducing machine "which was perfection," and which had been installed in several European mints, Hering decided the Mint's problems might stem from its use of an antiquated machine.

"It was a machine about forty years old and consequently very much out of date," he wrote. "I told Mr. Barber so but it made no impression on him, so I made my report to Mr. St. Gaudens who in turn told the President. Of course you can imagine what Teddy's feelings were on hearing the U.S.A. was so much out of date." [14]

The Mint soon replaced its out-of-date Hill machine with a Janvier lathe.

It didn't help, at least it didn't help Hering. Upon his return to the Mint Barber showed him "with great glee" a reduction of the $10 gold coin using the Janvier lathe. It was also poorly done. Hering reacted boldly, telling Barber that "a bad reduction can be made from a good machine," suggesting that maybe Barber wasn't sufficiently well-acquainted with the machine to make a good reduction. Hering said he was able to make the assertion knowing full well that he was right, having taken the precaution of having examples, in three different reliefs, prepared outside the mint by a Janvier lathe.

Saint-Gaudens' poor health, Hering writes, was likely behind the president's urging that the Mint go ahead with coinage. The Mint struck off several hundred high-relief specimens from the second modeling, which produced a wire rim and led to complaints from bankers about the inability of the coins to stack properly.

This, Hering charged, wouldn't have happened if the Mint had employed his third model in its original form, without the additional reduction made prior to its use for regular coinage.

Saint-Gaudens died on Aug. 3, 1907. His coins were released into circulation shortly thereafter.

Upset by the outcome of his strained negotiations with the Mint and the look of its low-relief product, Hering refused to give final approval to the designs, which meant that Saint-Gaudens' widow, Augusta, could not be paid. He relented at meeting with Mint officials in the spring of 1908, succumbing to pressure from Homer Saint-Gaudens and Augusta's lawyer.

Hering said he used the meeting to explain that he hadn't approved the gold $20 because the coin in circulation was not a good reduction of his third modeling. He showed his Janvier reductions of the $10 piece as proof. This was, however, to no avail.

An Irish lass

Since the coin's release many numismatic writers have taken on the task of relating the background of the gold double eagle.

The story that Mary Cunningham served as a model keeps coming to the forefront and is likely the most remembered by numismatists. This is perhaps because of statements by Homer Saint-Gaudens and a press dispatch from Harrisburg, Penn., dated Sept. 19, 1907. [15]

The dispatch reported that the Independent Order of Americans, which was holding its annual convention in Harrisburg, "has adopted a protest against the proposed placing of the face of Miss Mary Cunningham, the Irish-born girl, upon the United States gold coins, and has authorized the State Councilor to forward the protest to the United States Government at Washington."

The dispatch said that Cunningham, 26, a waitress in the town Cornish, near Windsor, Vt., was the model, explaining that Saint-Gaudens had had difficulty finding the proper model for the new coins, with "many beautiful girls rejected by him," before he found Cunningham on his summer stay in Cornish.

"She waited on him at table, and he almost immediately decided that hers was the face for the new coins," the dispatch said. Cunningham, who had come to the United States a few years prior, was reluctant, never having served as a model. "She simply let him copy her face because he was so very much in earnest."

Cunningham's "classic face," it said, was to appear on the cent, $10 gold piece and the $20 gold piece.

A cherished family story

Cunningham wasn't the only rumored model. Others have suggested that it was Davida Clark, Saint-Gaudens' mistress, or Alice Butler, said by Louise Hall Harp in *Saint-Gaudens and the Guilded Era* to have been the model for the profile head of the gold $10 coin. Another reference, often quickly passed over, was to the aforementioned "woman supposed to have negro blood in her veins."

It was within this comment by Homer Saint-Gaudens and an oft-told, cherished family story that truth may lay hidden.

The story that follows is the result of research by William E. Hagans, first published under his byline in the Feb. 26, 1991, issue of *Numismatic News*.

Hagans was drawn into the world of coin collecting and the background of the models for the Saint-Gaudens double eagle following the death of his mother in 1988. He and his sisters had come across an old photograph of a beautiful young woman, taken in the 1890s.

"We recalled that this was the cousin my grandmother often spoke of, who had posed for an important statue in New York and was represented on a gold coin," Hagans wrote. [16]

Also discovered was a sack of old coins. Hagans was charged with ascertaining the value, leading him to a fruitful "crash course in numismatics."

While identifying the gold coins within the bag, Hagans said he kept coming upon references to Saint-Gaudens and his gold coin designs.

"After I found Hettie Anderson's name on our family tree and her Manhattan street number in my grandmother's old address book, it was time to pursue the Saint-Gaudens' connection," he wrote. [17]

Hagans' big break in connecting Anderson to the *Sherman Monument* and the gold coin came when he obtained a copy of a book by John H. Dryfhout, curator of Aspet, the Saint-Gaudens National Historical Site in Cornish, N.H,. titled *The Work of Augustus Saint-Gaudens*. In it, Hagans found reference to Hettie Anderson (or "Cousin

***Two different views of Saint-Gaudens' Sherman Monument in New York.* Courtesy U.S. Department of the Interior, National Park Service, Saint-Gaudens National Historic Site, Cornish, N.H.**

Hettie Anderson, first model for Saint-Gaudens' Victory. Photo ca. 1890s. Courtesy Hagans Family Collection.

Tootie" as she is known within family circles) as being the first model for the head of *Victory* of Saint-Gaudens' *Sherman Monument.*

Dryfhout's heavily illustrated volume on the works of Augustus Saint-Gaudens shows a bust of Anderson by Saint-Gaudens, with Dryfhout's notation that it was the first head of *Victory*, and the one eventually employed. Inscribed on a label attached to the bust is: "First Sketch of Head/Victory/Sherman Monument" "To Hettie Anderson/AVGVSTVS Saint-Gavdens/1897."

Dryfhout adds that "Hettie Anderson was a New York model who posed for Saint-Gaudens." [18]

At the time his book was published, 1982, the whereabouts of the bust was not known.

Hagans had found his link to the important statue in New York and the gold coin told of in the old family story. Yet, he wondered, why hadn't anyone other than Dryfhout observed the connection?

According to Hagans, the answer lies in the deception of Homer Saint-Gaudens, who took charge after his father's death and, Hagans says, worked, as much as possible, to expunge from the record references to Davida Clark and obscure the possibility that an African-American served as a model for the $20 gold piece. [19]

That Homer Saint-Gaudens was aware that Anderson modeled for *Victory* is apparent from Anderson's response to a letter written by Homer Saint-Gaudens in August 1907, less than a week after his father's death, asking her to loan the bust so that a duplicate could be made.

Anderson replied in January of the following year that:

> "I rec'd your letter of the 9th asking me to loan, for the purpose of duplicating, the study of the head made from me, by Mr. Saint-Gaudens, when he first began the Sherman Group. When Mr. Saint-Gaudens gave me the head he . . . said: 'Some day this may be valuable to you, and if you will let me I will take it abroad and have it put in bronze for you, it may be worth a great deal of money.' I thanked him, but told him that I thought I would take it then — which I did. Valuing it as I do, and knowing as I do that it is the only one in existence, in that state — I am not willing to have any duplicates made of it, for any purpose whatever . . . (Dartmouth College Library.)" [20]

Hagans said his cousin's fear of duplication was not unfounded. A second head of *Victory* was copied in quantity and sold commercially.

The figure of Victory from the Sherman Monument. **Courtesy the Toledo Museum of Art.**

According to Hagans, the price Anderson paid for not giving in was to be left out of history as having been the first model for the head and torso of *Victory.*

In 1913 Homer Saint-Gaudens supervised the editing of his father's memoirs, renaming it *The Reminiscences of Augustus Saint-Gaudens* (this from his father's suggested *The Reminiscences of an Idiot*), leaving out Anderson's *Victory* bust from the "complete" catalog of his father's work, despite the fact that by that time it had been bronzed and placed on display, in 1908, at a memorial of the sculptor's work at New York's Metropolitan Museum of Art. [21]

Saint-Gaudens spoke glowingly of Anderson in the uncensored version of the *Idiot* memoirs. Saint-Gaudens wrote:

"I . . . modeled . . . the nude for the figure of Victory of the Sherman group, from certainly the handsomest model I have ever seen of either sex, and I have seen a great many . . . The model was a young woman from Georgia [actually, South Carolina, born in 1873], dark long legged, which is not common with women, and which if not exaggerated, is an essential requirement for beauty; Besides she had what is also rare with handsome models, a power of posing patiently, steadily and thoroughly in the spirit one wished. She could be depended on . . . Having seen her the other day for the first time in eight years, I found her just as splendid as she was fifteen years ago when she was first drawn to my attention . . . (Dartmouth College Library.)"[22]

In February 1897 Saint-Gaudens reported to his niece, Rose Nichols, that work was progressing rapidly with his *Victory* model. He also mentioned that Swedish artist Anders Zorn had made an etching of him and of his model during a rest period.

"The etching is a beautiful representation of the obviously tired, middle-aged sculptor, his distinctive leonine features half obscured by shade, and the vibrant young model reclining nude in the background, surrounded by Zorn's swirling lines," Hagans wrote. "It has been assumed by some that the model was Davida, his mistress, but the resemblance to Hettie Anderson is unmistakable." [23]

According to Hagans, the same letter appears in Homer Saint-Gaudens' version of the memoirs, including the reference to the model, but with the substitution of a Zorn etching produced a year later in Paris. The published etching shows Saint-Gaudens' *Puritan* statue in the background, not his model for *Victory.*

The bust of Hettie Anderson by Augustus Saint-Gaudens, used in preparation of his Victory for the Sherman Monument. Photograph by Lawrence Chamberlain.

Ten years after Zorn's etchings were made, Augustus Saint-Gaudens wrote to the artist in August 1906:

> "Your masterpiece of me hangs in my study and is a constant pleasure; I wish I could really repay you for it. You know I promised you a reduction of my nude of the Goddess-like Miss Anderson, but . . . it was destroyed in the fire [of 1904 at Cornish] . . . (Zorn Collections, Mora, Sweden.)" [24]

Hagans said the "only veiled allusion" to Hettie Anderson made by Homer Saint-Gaudens was his mention of a woman with Negro blood. Homer Saint-Gaudens had written of the model:

> "The profile head Saint-Gaudens modeled in relief from a bust originally intended for the Sherman Victory, adding the feathers upon the President's suggestion. Many persons knew it as the 'Mary Cunningham' design, because posed for by an Irish maid, when only a 'pure American' should have served for a model for our national coin. As a matter of fact, the so-called features of the Irish girl appear scarcely the size of a pinhead upon the full-length Liberty, the body of which was posed for by a Swede. Also, the modern American blue blood may delight in the discovery that the profile head was modeled from a woman supposed to have negro blood in her veins. Who other than an Indian may be a 'pure American' is undetermined." [25]

According to Hagans, although quite fair, his cousin was indeed black.

Additional research conducted by Hagans into the letters of Adolph Weinman led to the discovery of a highly suggestive letter written by Augustus Saint-Gaudens during the time period in which Saint-Gaudens was hard at work on the double eagle design. Dated Jan. 2, 1906, it reads:

(Facing page) The Anders Zorn etching of Augustus Saint-Gaudens and the model for Victory (New York, 1897). Though some have argued that it depicts Saint-Gaudens' mistress Davida Clark, William Hagans believes it is of his cousin Hettie Anderson. This would seem to be supported by a 1906 letter to Zorn from Saint-Gaudens discovered by Hagans in the Zorn Collections in Mora, Sweden. **Courtesy of the U.S. Department of the Interior, National Park Service, Saint-Gaudens National Historic Site, Cornish, N.H.**

133

"Dear Weinman: Will you please mail the enclosed letter to Miss Anderson. Perhaps if she is posing for you, you might let her go for one, two or three days, I need her badly . . . " (26)

Though not conclusive, Saint-Gaudens' call for Anderson to serve again as a model is interesting in light of Homer Saint-Gaudens' claim that a Swedish woman, likely Davida Clark, served as the model for the torso.

According to Hagans, by the 1890s Augustus Saint-Gaudens' affair with Clark and the resulting child had been discovered by the sculptor's wife, Augusta, and "Davida was exiled to Darien, Conn." Although the sculptor occasionally saw Davida and their son, Louis P. Clark, "her posing for the double eagle is highly doubtful, especially given his grave illness and the watchfulness of Augusta." (27)

'Victory' bust recovered

In 1990, with Dryfhout's help, the Hagans were fortunate to recover the missing *Victory* bust of Hettie Anderson. Hagans wrote:

"When my wife [Willow] and I visited the Saint-Gaudens National Historic Site in Cornish, N.H., in summer 1988, Mr. Dryfhout's first words in reference to Anderson were that he had been looking for the bust of her for the last 20 years. In his exhaustive cataloging of the sculptor's work, Hettie's bust was one of the few works whose location remained a mystery." (28)

In early 1990 Dryfhout informed Hagans that the bust had surfaced and was going on auction at Christie's in New York. Hagans and his wife purchased the bust and say that, in time, they plan to donate it to the National Historic Site in New Hampshire, where the bust of Hettie Anderson can take "her rightful place among the sculptor's magnificent creations."

Chapter 9

Godless coins

Teddy Roosevelt and the motto 'In God We Trust'

The battle over the use of the motto "In God We Trust" on U.S. currency is a never ending one. Just about each and every year suit is filed in Federal court by those who object its use, and each and every year they are defeated.

In the early 1900s, however, debate raged not because of its placement on U.S. coins but its deletion, as protests were raised over the release of the "godless" gold $10 eagle and $20 double eagle designed by Augustus Saint-Gaudens.

The oft-told story is that President Theodore Roosevelt objected to the use of the deity on a coin as being sacrilegious. It was, therefore, omitted from the 1907 and some 1908 eagles as well as the 1907 double eagles.

Although it is true that Roosevelt issued a lengthy statement defending the decision to leave the religious motto off the new gold coins, this was only part of the story — a story of an artist who believed simplicity of design essential and of a president who defended this position.

Motto's first use

The motto "In God We Trust" was first introduced on U.S. coins with the two-cent piece of 1864. Its placement there is credited to Rev. W.R. Watkinson, minister of the gospel, Ridleyville, Pa., who

Rev. W.R. Watkinson was the first to suggest the use of a religious motto on U.S. coins. In a Nov. 13, 1861, letter to Treasury Secretary Salmon P. Chase, Watkinson called for the placement of the words "God, Liberty and Law" on the nation's coinage.

suggested honoring the deity, in some form, on the nation's currency.

Watkinson wrote in a Nov. 13, 1861, letter to Treasury Secretary Salmon P. Chase that:

> "You are about to submit your annual report to Congress respecting the affairs of the national finances.
>
> One fact touching our currency has hitherto been seriously overlooked. I mean the recognition of the Almighty God in some form in our coins." [1]

Watkinson worried that if the nation was shattered beyond reconstruction by the Civil War that antiquaries of following centuries, looking at the nation's coins, would conclude that the United States was a heathen nation.

> "What I propose is that instead of the goddess of liberty, we shall have next inside the 13 stars a ring inscribed with the words 'perpetual union;' within this ring the all-seeing eye, crowned with a halo; beneath this eye the American flag, bearing in its field stars to the number of States united; in the folds of the bars the words 'God, liberty, law.' " [2]

Chase agreed, in principle, writing to Mint Director James Pollock on Nov. 20, 1861, and calling for placement of "a motto expressing in

Several variations were tried before the motto "In God We Trust" was selected.

the fewest and tersest words possible this national recognition." [3]

Several variations of the motto were proposed and tried by Mint engraver James B. Longacre, including "Our Trust is in God," "God Our Trust," "God Trust," and "God is our Trust."

It wasn't, however, until a Dec. 9, 1963, letter from Chase to Pollock in regard to the new two-cent coin that Chase suggested "In God We Trust" be used. Failing this, he proposed "God is Our Shield."

Following its first use on the two-cent piece, an act passed in 1865 allowed the Mint director to place the motto "In God We Trust" on U.S. coins at his discretion. In 1866 it was added to all silver and gold coins, with the exception of the dime, half dime and three-cent piece, which were omitted due to size. Use of the motto was continued by the Coinage Act of 1873 and eventually adopted for lower-denomination U.S. coins.

The price of omission

In 1905 President Theodore Roosevelt commissioned renowned sculptor Augustus Saint-Gaudens to take on the task of redesigning the nation's gold coinage.

Saint-Gaudens asked the legal requirements concerning the motto "In God We Trust" and other inscriptions in a Nov. 22, 1905, letter to Treasury Secretary L.M. Shaw, enclosing a copy to Roosevelt. Saint-Gaudens observed that law required an impression "emblematic of liberty, with the inscription of the word 'liberty' and the year of coinage" and asked if he could add the word "justice" or "law" to his design. He also queried whether authorization was in place requiring the placement of "In God We Trust" on the coinage.[4]

Shaw's reply is unknown, though it's likely that no objection to the omission of the motto was forwarded to the artist, even though legal requirements existed.

Roosevelt, likewise, made no reference to Saint-Gaudens' concerns regarding the motto, saying only of Saint-Gaudens' design:

> "This is first class. I have no doubt we can get permission to put on the word 'Justice,' and I firmly believe that you can evolve something that will not only be beautiful from the artistic standpoint, but that, between the very high relief of the Greek and the very low relief of the modern coins, will be adapted both to the mechanical necessities of our mint production and the needs of modern commerce, and yet will be worthy of a civilized people — which is not true of our present coins." [5]

Saint-Gaudens had written to Roosevelt years earlier (in relation to his design for Roosevelt's inaugural medal) that simplicity of inscription was preferable in artistic designs. He apparently felt similarly in his work on the new gold coins. [6]

His son, Homer Saint-Gaudens, related in a 1920 article for *Century Illustrated Monthly Magazine* that the problem of including the authorized inscriptions was a difficult one, requiring the use of a date on each coin, the word "Liberty," "E Pluribus Unum," the legend "In God We Trust," inclusion of 13 stars to represent the original colonies, 46 stars for the states then in the Union and "United States of America." Homer Saint-Gaudens wrote:

> "The suggestion of the word 'Justice' was given up. In the case of the twenty-dollar gold piece the thirteen stars and the 'E. Pluribus Unum,' and in the case of the ten-dollar gold piece the forty-six stars, were placed upon the previously milled edges of the coin. The 'In God we trust' was discarded as an inartistic intrusion not required by law. The President gave his sanction to placing the date of the coinage in Roman instead of Arabic figures. The word 'Liberty,' the denomination of the coin, and the 'United States of America' alone remained to be dealt with. The situation seemed clarified.
>
> Unfortunately, however, the removal of the 'In God we trust' drew down the lightning of public disapproval. The burden of the complaint was that the dropping of the legend was irreligious, although in this connection it was amusing to discover that Salmon P. Chase, who was Lincoln's secretary of the treasury, sustained quite as stern a censure for placing these words upon the coins as was aroused by their removal. The President, with his usual

The two-cent piece of 1864 was the first U.S. coin released into circulation carrying the "In God We Trust" motto. The motto was quickly added to other denominations.

Augustus Saint-Gaudens, designer of the gold $10 and $20 coins released in 1907, considered simplicity essential in coinage design. The motto "In God We Trust" was thereby left off the first issues of both denominations. It was restored by Congress.

delight in a fight, took the onus of this charge upon himself and stood the tempest remarkably well; but at a later date, the sculptor being dead, and Mr. Roosevelt no longer in a position to prevent it, the authorities in the mint reverted to their own sweet way, with the result that 'In God we trust' and the Arabic numerals reappeared on the Saint-Gaudens's coins, to the increased impairment of whatever of worth in the original design had been allowed to remain." [7]

Roosevelt reacts

Publicly Roosevelt defended the position, saying in a Nov. 13, 1907, letter that:

"When the question of the new coinage came up we looked into the law and found there was no warrant for putting 'In God We Trust' on the coins. As the custom, although without legal warrant has grown up, however, I might have felt at liberty to keep the inscription had I approved of its being on the coinage. But as I did not approve of it, I did not direct that it should again be put on.

Of course the matter of the law is absolutely in the hands of congress and any direction of congress in the matter will be immediately obeyed. At present as I have said, there is no warrant in law for inscription.

My own feeling in the matter is due to my very firm conviction that to put such a motto on coins or to use it in any kindred manner, not only does no good but does positive harm, and is in effect irreverence which comes dangerously close to sacrilege. A beautiful and solemn sentence such as the one in question should be treated and uttered with that fine reverence which necessarily implies a certain exaltation of spirit.

Any use which tends to cheapen it, and above all, any use which tends to secure its being treated in a spirit of levity, is from every standpoint profoundly to be regretted. It is a motto which is indeed well to have inscribed in our great national monuments, in our temples of justice, in our legislative halls, and in buildings such as those at West Point and Annapolis — in short, wherever it will tend to arouse and inspire a lofty emotion in those who look thereon. But it seems to me eminently unwise to cheapen

President Theodore Roosevelt took the brunt of the criticism for the omission of "In God We Trust" from the U.S. gold coinage of 1907. Roosevelt said, "My own feeling in the matter is due to my very firm conviction that to put such a motto on coins or to use it in any kindred manner, not only does no good but does positive harm, and is in effect irreverence which comes close to sacrilege."

it by use on postage stamps, or in advertisements.

As regards its use on coinage, we have actual experience by which to go. In all my life I have never heard any human being speak reverently of this motto on the coins, or show any sign of its having appealed to any high emotion in him, but I have literally hundreds of times heard it used as an occasion of, and incitement to the sneering ridicule which it is above all things undesirable that so beautiful and exalted a phrase should excite.

For example, throughout the long contest extending over several decades on the free coinage question, the existence of this motto on the coins was a constant source of jest and ridicule; and this was unavoidable. Everyone must remember the innumerable cartoons and articles based on phrases like 'In God We Trust for the Eight Cents,' 'In God We Trust for the Short Weight,' 'In God We Trust for the Thirty-seven Cents We do not Pay,' etc., etc. Surely I am well within bounds when I say that a use of the phrase which invites constant levity of this type is most undesirable. If congress alters the law and directs me to replace on the coins the sentence in question, the direction will be immediately put into effect, but I very earnestly trust that the religious sentiment of the country, the spirit of reverence in the country will prevent any such action being taken." [8]

Roosevelt was wrong. On May 18, 1908, Congress passed an act requiring the motto's restoration. Today it continues to appear on U.S. coins and has found a place on the nation's paper money as well.

Chapter 10

A nation's dime

Acclaimed sculptor Dr. Selma Burke says she designed the dime. Tradition says credit should go to Mint engraver John Sinnock. Who's right?

Did John R. Sinnock design the Roosevelt dime or did Dr. Selma H. Burke? At first glance this might seem like an easy question to answer.

Tradition holds that former Mint chief engraver John R. Sinnock designed the coin now used by millions of Americans. His initials appear on it, and all credit has gone to him in the past and likely will continue to do so in the future. But is this right? Or is it possible that Burke, 94, an immensely captivating and renowned sculptor is correct in her unending belief that Sinnock plagiarized her design from a life-study she did of President Franklin D. Roosevelt in the early 1940s, giving her no credit whatsoever?

Marked success

Frankly, the passage of time has made discovering what is the truth in the question of Dr. Burke's claim virtually impossible. Many of the principals and potential witnesses to what may have been an

Dr. Selma H. Burke at her studio in Pennsylvania. Depicted in the photograph she holds is her work Peace, *a woman comforting a dove with broken wing. Despite being largely confined to a wheelchair, Burke, 94, remains active at her art and teaching.* **Photograph by the author.**

injustice against one of the nation's leading sculptors have passed on.

Also, given the fact that Burke is black, many have discounted any claim she may have to the design purely on the basis of her skin color. This is a shame and an injustice of its own, but it's how this story has been viewed by some.

Yet even those who elect to dismiss Dr. Burke's claim, either upon a simplistic judgement made on the basis of race or because of absence of definitive proof, would have to admit that in Burke there is a story of marked success — a story of a woman who went up against remarkable odds to come out on top. It is an interesting story in its own right and worthy of retelling.

There is the delightful personal account of a lady who met with the president, charmed him, modeled him from life and used this work as a stepping stone to a career matched by few and replete with major awards and accomplishments. Also, there is the story of a genuinely warm, charming person who honestly, and deeply, believes that she has been wronged and would like to set the record straight.

Perhaps, above all, there is the story of the coin and the need to re-examine what we know and don't know of its creation — if for no other reason than to offer the numismatic community additional food for thought and to bring home the point that history is not chiseled in stone. There's often room for legitimate speculation when it comes to what is regarded as fact.

How Burke enters the picture and how she came to the solid conviction that credit for designing the Roosevelt dime belongs to her was explored by this writer in an extensive interview in July 1993 at Burke's studio in Pennsylvania.

Faithful portrayal

To fully tell the story we must, however, begin at an earlier point, following Roosevelt's death on April 12, 1945, when efforts began to honor him on a coin. The idea was to have the coin designed, engraved, and ready to place into circulation in conjunction with the March of Dimes campaign the following year. The president had been afflicted by polio and proceeds from the March of Dimes campaign went to fight the disease.

Work on the new dime design, which would replace Adolph Weinman's Winged Liberty or Mercury motif (minted since 1916), began immediately. On Oct. 12, 1945, Sinnock submitted models to Acting Mint Director Leland Howard, who sent the models to the Commission of Fine Arts.

Photos of these early models, and additional details of the commission's reaction to Sinnock's design, can be found in Don Taxay's *U.S. Mint and Coinage: An Illustrated History From 1776 to the Present.*

Taxay quotes commission chairman Gilmore Clarke, who complained in an Oct. 22, 1945, letter to Howard that the modeling of Roosevelt's head was not good and that it needed more dignity. Clarke wrote, "It may be that the position of the head — the angle at which it is placed on the background — and the shape and ending of the neck are at fault." [1]

Mint Chief Engraver John R. Sinnock with a model for the Roosevelt dime. Sinnock is most often credited with the design for the coin.

The commission also made suggestions for changes to the reverse design and preferred a modeling of a torch with branches on each side rather than another showing a hand holding a torch.

Sinnock reworked the models for the obverse, which were again submitted and again rejected. The commission suggested a competition be held among five prominent artists (Edward McCartan, James Earle Fraser, Paul Manship, Adolph A. Weinman and Jo Davidson) to obtain a better design. This was rejected, however, because of the short time frame set for introduction of the new coin. [2]

Official announcement of the new coin was made from the White House by President Harry S. Truman and Franklin D. Roosevelt Jr. on Jan. 30, 1946 — what would have been the late president's 64th birthday.

The new dime was readily accepted by the public and generally praised. Its adoption was another step in a conversion from allegorical designs; only the half dollar remained.

Writing of the dime's design, Cornelius Vermeule, in his *Numismatic Art in America: Aesthetics of the United States Coinage*, was effusive over its portrayal of Roosevelt. Vermeule wrote, "He

The new dime was released into circulation in 1946. Official announcement of its release was made from the White House on Jan. 30 by President Harry S. Truman and Franklin D. Roosevelt Jr.

[Sinnock] demonstrated his long practice and superior craftsmanship as a die-designer in producing a clean, satisfying, and modestly stylish, no-nonsense coin that in total view comes forth with notes of grandeur." [3]

Vermeule then compared Sinnock's work to that of 18th century French sculptor Jeane Antoine Houdon, who had sculpted a famed bust of Washington from life.

"Houdon never modeled Roosevelt in clay and plaster nor carved him in marble, but had he done so the results would have surely resembled the profile on the dime," Vermeule said. "The die-designer has achieved a precise, detailed portrait which shows full force of character amid a faithful portrayal." [4]

The comparison to Houdon is interesting, if only because the French sculptor comes into play in Burke's story of how she came to model Roosevelt and ultimately claim credit for the dime's design.

'Then some'

Born in Mooresville, N.C., on Dec. 31, 1900, Burke gained her entrance to Roosevelt's inner sanctum by winning an art competition in 1943, sponsored by the Fine Arts Commission for the District of Columbia.

Dr. Burke's Pennsylvania studio and home. The walls of her studio are covered with letters from famous personages including those she received from Franklin D. Roosevelt. **Photo courtesy of August Swain.**

Burke was in a Staten Island, N.Y., hospital, recovering from a back injury sustained as a truck driver for the Navy, when she learned that she had won the competition, which called for her to prepare a profile of Roosevelt for a plaque to be placed in the Recorder of Deeds building in Washington, D.C. The notice that she won had been sent some time earlier, but, as Burke was laid up with her injury, had gone unnoticed in her accumulating mail at her New York apartment.

A friend eventually checked her mail, and doctors worked to get her back on her feet so she could complete a design by the pre-set deadline. With the help of friends, she obtained several pictures of the president but found few that could be used.

"When I tried to find profiles of him, he was always with three-quarters of his face and smiling," Burke said. "So there weren't many profiles of him. I couldn't find [any] at that time. I had gone through all of the logs in the *New York Times*, every New York paper and every book.

"He was very popular and was photographed all over, but there was nothing that I could use that I saw. So I had to do a composite of what I thought he looked like in the first one.

"But, my father had a saying: 'You have to do all you can and then some. It is the 'then some' that is going to get you where you want to go.' " [5]

Burke said that, when she entered the competition to design the plaque for the new Recorder of Deeds building in Washington, D.C., she found it difficult to find profiles of the president. Most photographs showed him three-quarters face and smiling.

Burke decided she hadn't done all she could, so she wrote to the president:

> ". . . [I] asked him if he would see me. I told him I was a student at Columbia and I had studied the background of Mr. Houdon, who was a French sculptor who had done the president, President Washington — the quarter that we have. And it took him [Houdon] two months to come to America . . . and that the best bust of Washington was done by Houdon.
>
> I said, 'You know, Mr. President, I am about four hours by train from Washington and I am two hours by plane.' And, I said, 'I have a Ford automobile and I could be down there in five or six hours in my Ford automobile if you would see me just for a few minutes so I could make some sketches.' "

Roosevelt agreed to meet with her.

'Four Freedoms'

A model for sculptor Manship and others, Burke cut a stylish figure, arriving at the White House decked out in a grey-striped suit, sporting an umbrella and portfolio — an image interrupted only by a roll of brown butcher's paper she had acquired from an A&P grocery store on which to draw.

"When I came in, he was sitting there, you know, in his wheelchair, and he had his hand out," she said of her first meeting with Roosevelt. "I thought I'd never get to it. Anyway, we shook hands and I started taking off my coat and putting down my things.

"I was just in a hurry, because he said he was going to give me 45 minutes and I wanted to use that 45 minutes making sketches. So I took off my things and threw everything off but my hat and I just started to draw him. In the meantime, he was asking me all of these questions . . . we just got on beautifully."

They talked about Roosevelt's home and shared a common acquaintance in Peace Mission movement leader Father Divine, who ran an inexpensive New York kitchen Burke frequented during her days of teaching art as part of the Work Progress Administration's efforts in Harlem.

"But all the time, I'm trying to talk to him and I am trying to draw . . . so that certain parts of his face were done well and certain parts were done badly," she said. "So I had to start over again. That is

Aged and tattered, the original drawing of President Franklin D. Roosevelt by Burke on brown butcher's paper is maintained in a frame at her studio. The drawing, prepared from private sittings with the president, served as the basis for her Four Freedoms *plaque.* Photograph by the author.

Two photographs of Burke's Four Freedoms. *The enlargement of the plaque provides a better representation of Burke's likeness of President Franklin D. Roosevelt as it appears in final form. (The marks of damage are on the print, not the plaque.) The second photograph is of August Swain with the* Four Freedoms *plaque, located in the lobby of the Recorder of Deeds building at 505 D Street N.W., Washington, D.C.* Courtesy of August Swain.

154

when I got up and took his head and said, 'Would you just hold like this for a few minutes.' " Roosevelt did.

She would go back a second time and continue her modeling. Over the years of her acquaintance with Roosevelt, she collected 35 letters between her and the president, which she cherishes and proudly displays.

Burke also fondly remembers a visit from First Lady Eleanor Roosevelt on the morning of March 6, 1945. Mrs. Roosevelt had come to view the drawing.

Burke's sister made breakfast, using fine silver passed down through the family and originally received, Burke says, by her grandfather from Stonewall Jackson.

"And I had a card table, and my aunt had made a very, very beautiful little handmade tablecloth," Burke said. "My sister served cranberry juice; most people weren't drinking it then.

"We had the Roosevelt profile over on my easel. I had a special easel. So we pulled the cord and everybody went 'ah,' except Mrs. Roosevelt. She just kept looking and looking."

She told Burke that it looked like Roosevelt but complained, "You have made him very young."

"That is when I started giving her a lecture," Burke said. "I was much more of a professorial type then than I am now. I've learned to be gentle with people, no matter who they are."

She told Mrs. Roosevelt: "No, I've done it for tomorrow and tomorrow. I don't want the people [to] feel something about a wrinkled old man. I want to give the feeling of a strong Roman gladiator that we could feel was strong and would lead our country."

Mrs. Roosevelt asked Burke if she would like another sitting with the president. Burke agreed. Plans were made for an additional 45 minutes of modeling to take place on April 20 while the president was in San Francisco attending a conference, but the president died before the meeting could occur.

"So I never bothered the drawing anymore," she said. "I just finished that plaque, that relief, and had it in the show [at the Modern Age Gallery, July 1945]."

Her work on the drawing at the White House drew the attention of major magazines and newspapers, Burke said, including the *Washington Post, Time* and *Life.* But, she said, she shunned this because she wanted recognition for the finished work not her visits with the president.

She did receive notice in *Time* magazine for the drawing and again when the plaque was officially unveiled on Sept. 24, 1945.

President Harry S. Truman was on hand for the official dedication of the plaque, saying of her depiction Roosevelt, "you got him as we knew him at his best."

Reporting on the unveiling, the Sept. 25, 1945, issue of the Washington, D.C. *Evening Star* said the $750 plaque, known as the *Four Freedoms*, had been commissioned by the District Commissioners in July 1943 for the new $450,000 Recorder of Deeds building at Sixth and D streets N.W. Ground for the structure had been broken in September 1940 by President Roosevelt.

The plaque was unveiled by Frederick S. Weaver, deputy recorder of deeds, great grandson of abolitionist Frederick Douglass. Douglass had served as the first black recorder of deeds in Washington, D.C., and as a district commissioner. The ceremony was presided over by Marshal L. Shepard, recorder of deeds, who explained that the plaque was the dream of Dr. William J. Tompkins, former recorder of deeds. Burke is shown in a photograph with Truman, the plaque, and Shepard.

The ceremony featured speeches, radio vocalists, performances by the Metropolitan Police Band and the official presentation of the bronze *Four Freedoms* plaque by Rep. William L. Dawson, D-Ill., to Commissioner John Russell Young. [6]

Burke, the artist

This was the first in a string of major achievements in what was to be a long and distinguished art career that did not come to fruition until later in life. Burke first trained for a medical career and spent some time as a surgeon's technician at St. Agnes School of Nursing in Raleigh, N.C.

It was during a stint as a private nurse in a wealthy New York home in the late 1920s that she gained exposure to high culture, visiting the opera on numerous occasions with her wealthy employer and working as a model for such notables as Manship; Edward Steichen, a pioneer in photography as an art form; and Alfred Stieglitz, a prominent photo-engraver. It was these influences, she said, that eventually turned her attention to art.

In 1935 she won the Rosewald Foundation Fellowship. One year later she was awarded the Boehler Foundation Fellowship. The fellowships allowed her to travel to Europe, where she studied with French painter Henri Matisse and sculptor Aristide Maillol.

She left Europe a few months before Hitler invaded Austria and returned to New York where, in 1941, she earned a master of fine arts degree from Columbia University.

In 1970, at the age of 70, she received a doctorate in arts and letters from Livingstone College, Salisbury, N.C. It is only one in a lengthy list of credits that includes an additional doctorate, in teaching, and numerous honorary degrees.

A younger Burke (ca. 1950s) with an unfinished walnut sculpting of Uplift *completed in 1956. The sculpture shows a moving scene of a mother and children huddling together during a Southern lynching.* Courtesy of August Swain.

Burke also founded the Selma Burke School of Sculpture in New York and the Selma Burke Art Center in Pittsburgh. She is a recognized poet and has had an algebra problem published in a major mathematics book.

Burke has lectured at Harvard, Swarthmore, Livingstone and other colleges and has been singled out for her outstanding achievements by the governors of Pennsylvania and North Carolina. In Pennsylvania she was honored with the Distinguished Daughter of Pennsylvania award. Past recipients have included Princess Grace of Monaco, Pearl S. Buck, and Mamie Eisenhower.

In October 1990 a major four-month exhibit of her works opened at the Lyndon Baines Johnson Library and Museum, part of the University of Texas, and was viewed by an estimated 90,000 people.

Among more than 1,000 of her sculptures gracing college campuses, museums and private collections is a moving bronze statue, *Uplift*, relating a disturbing scene of a mother and her children huddling close together during a lynching — a piece that links directly to Burke's past.

A bronze example of this statue was donated in 1991

to Hillship Township, W.Va., in honor of the 100th anniversary of the birth of Pulitzer Prize winning author Pearl S. Buck. An additional version was presented to Spellman College in 1993.

Also by Burke are the *John Brown Memorial* in Lake Placid, N.Y., a bust of Booker T. Washington for the Federal government, a bronze of Dr. Martin Luther King, and a bust of Duke Ellington.

High praise

A 1990-dated proclamation from Pennsylvania Gov. Robert P. Casey praises Burke, saying:

An accomplished sculptor, Burke has won most major art awards. Shown are her bronze Mother and Child *and* Elizabeth Cartwright *sculptures created in 1951.* Courtesy of August Swain.

"You have had the opportunity to travel around the world studying under such world-famous artists as Henri Matisse and Reis. You have helped young people develop an appreciation for the arts. And your leadership and compassion for those you work with will continue to produce future artists.

You have captured the essence of greatness, of sorrow, of love and of humanity in your works. Your sensitivity is evident in your statue of Dr. Martin Luther King Jr., the bronze bust of Duke Ellington, and the portrait of President Franklin D. Roosevelt.

Your ten cents can be found in every community across the nation. But that dime is worth so much more than its monetary value. By sculpting President Roosevelt, you preserved for all time an artistic talent that reflects our history and, at the same time, generates pride in the African-American culture."

Another who praised her for work on the dime was FDR's son, James, who wrote to Burke on Sept. 16, 1990, from Newport Beach, Calif., saying:

"When my father, Franklin Delano Roosevelt, was elected president in 1933, he had a vision of a government that would provide the most basic of needs to its people. His presidency spanned 12 years, a time during which the quality of life was improved for all Americans, not just a privileged few. The bust of him you created serves as a reminder of his vision. Its imprint on the U.S. dime is representative not only of his achievements, but yours, as well.

Although Americans may not recognize the name or face of the person who sculpted it, the face of my father on the U.S. dime is a constant testimonial to a great man who envisioned a great country. With my deepest gratitude and that of my family, we thank you for that memory and congratulate you on this wonderful exhibition."

But even though governors, FDR's relatives and others of note have come to accept Burke's claims of having designed the dime, few within the numismatic world have credited her with doing so. Her story has appeared sporadically in numismatic circles over the years, with only limited support. Chief among those who have followed her background is Edward C. Rochette, a prolific numismatic writer and former American Numismatic Association president.

September 16, 1990

Dr. Selma Burke
c/o The Kingsley Association
Pittsburgh, Pennsylvania 15213

Dear Dr. Burke:

It is with great honor and pleasure that I commend you
on your life achievements in the world of art. Your
dedication and skill in preserving the history of these
United States is a gift of the highest order.

When my father, Franklin Delano Roosevelt, was elected
president in 1933, he had a vision of a government that
would provide the most basic of needs to its people.
His presidency spanned 12 years, a time during which the
quality of life was improved for all Americans, not just
a privileged few. The bust of him you created serves as
a reminder of his vision. Its imprint on the U.S. dime
is representative not only of his achievements, but yours,
as well.

Although Americans may not recognize the name or face of
the person who sculpted it, the face of my father on the
U.S. dime is a constant testimonial to a great man who
envisioned a great country. With my deepest gratitude
and that of my family, we thank you for that memory and
congratulate you on this wonderful exhibition.

Every good wish.

Sincerely,

James Roosevelt

James Roosevelt

JR:cf

JAMES ROOSEVELT & COMPANY

NEWPORT CENTER
567 SAN NICOLAS DRIVE • SUITE 106 • NEWPORT BEACH, CALIFORNIA 92660 • FAX 714/720-9476
714/720-7484

A Sept. 16, 1990, letter from Franklin D. Roosevelt's son James to Burke commending her for her artistic achievements, including the Roosevelt dime. **Courtesy of August Swain.**

Rochette, who graciously provided his file of background material as reference, has argued in her favor. In a *Los Angeles Times* article, maintained as part of his file, he wrote of the modeling of the president:

> ". . . that [Burke's] image was soon to become the most prolifically issued image the world would know of FDR. To many, it was the portrait plagiarized by the U.S. Mint for the design of the Roosevelt dime.
>
> Some argue that Roosevelt's features are so distinctive that all profile portraits of the president will be similar. Circumstantial or not, all one has to do is to compare the preliminary sketches prepared by Sinnock to the portrait on display at the Hall of Records.
>
> Sinnock's initial designs not only bore remarkable similarity, but his suggested reverse featured a representation of the Four Freedoms — not unlike that featured on Burke's plaque."

Asking, "Did history repeat itself in 1945?", Rochette explained that it wouldn't be the first time Sinnock was charged with numismatic plagiarism.

John Sinnock has been charged by numerous writers for plagiarism in regard to the 1926 Sesquicentennial half dollar. His initials appear on the coin which bears a portrayal of George Washington and Calvin Coolidge from sketches by John Frederick Lewis.

In 1925 Mint employee Sinnock had submitted designs for the Sesquicentennial of Independence half dollar. The sponsoring commission rejected them and hired artist John Frederick Lewis to redesign the coin. Lewis' sketches were accepted by the Commission of Fine Arts and appear on the coin, which bears Sinnock's initials and makes no mention of Lewis.

Late night call

According to Burke, history did repeat itself. She says that she received a call late one night from Ruth Wilson, a secretary at the Recorder of Deeds office, urging her to come to Washington, saying that her drawing was being sent to the Mint for use in designing the dime.

"The reason why I knew that Mr. Sinnock had gotten it from there was that Ruth Wilson had called me in the middle of the night, in New York, to tell me that this man, Sinnock, and Marshall Shepard were making a deal and that he had taken the drawing to the Mint," Burke said. "Ruth Wilson said, 'You'd better come to Washington because Marshall Shepard and Sinnock are doing a thing on you.' "

According to Burke, Wilson and herself were godparents to the daughter of a Mary Wilson.

"She [Ruth Wilson] felt very close and she had to let me know what was going on," Burke said. "I was sleeping, and I said, 'I am not going to Washington. I won this thing.' No, I just took a stand."

Burke also believes that part of the reason she has never received full credit for the design was the politics of the period. She thinks the change in administration from Democrat to Republican, which affected the leadership at the Recorder of Deeds office, had some impact on proper credit not being accorded to her. The plaque had been the idea of a Democrat to honor a Democratic president, and Shepard was a Republican.

"So I am sure that it was because there was no one watching what was going on," she said, "and because they found out I was black. That was definitely one of the things at that particular time. The material that I sent, when they let the competition, had nothing to do with race. I had done many white people.

"I was a student at Columbia and I did a bust of William Allen and of Charlie Schwab, the financier." It was, she said, such work that won her the commission, not her race.

Burke maintains that her subsequent attempts to gain credit for the dime led J. Edgar Hoover to launch an FBI investigation into her activities. Considering Hoover's known predilection for keeping tabs on anyone and everyone even slightly off the beaten path, and the obsessive fear of communism in that era, this not all that unlikely.

Not helping the cause, she said, was that she once carried a banner in a New York parade that advocated freedom of press and other civil liberties but was tagged by some as socialist in bent.

"My husband [Claude McKay] was a very well-known writer," Burke said. "And he said, 'Well, I don't want to get mixed up in that [communism], but I would sure like to march in that parade.' So I said, 'I'll march.'

"So I was in this communist parade from 14th Street to 59th Street carrying a banner, a big thing, 'I am for free press.' It was the only way the newspapers could be in that parade, because they didn't want to get in a parade of communism to get their fight over.

"But I could, because I wasn't anything but just an ordinary citizen who wanted the press free. Everything was so separated and segregated that one didn't think about that communist thing."

Whether or not she became the target of an FBI investigation is largely a moot point when it comes to the story of the dime, though it now frames some of her mind-set concerning who she blames for her drawing being used without proper attribution. Since then, Burke has waged a low-key campaign to be recognized as the coin's designer, highlighted by a 1994 appearance on *CBS Sunday Morning* with Charles Osgood.

She remains largely in the background, as others, including curator and friend August Swain, work to assemble her memoirs and gain recognition wherever they can. But it is an unfunded and largely unheralded effort that has had limited impact. Too much time has passed, and documentation is slim.

Open to question

Also, legitimate arguments can be offered in rebuttal. For instance, just because Sinnock has been charged with artistic plagiarism in regard to the 1926 Sesquicentennial half dollar doesn't automatically condemn him in relation to the dime.

An article in the March 1946 issue of *Numismatic Scrapbook Magazine* says Sinnock claimed to have used two life-studies he did of Roosevelt during 1933-1934 for the dime and consulted photos of the president. [7]

Sinnock did his own studies of Roosevelt from life in the early 1930s, as shown by a Mint inaugural medal. The same Roosevelt portrait was used for this memorial medal issued by the Mint after the president's death.

Sinnock did prepare studies of Roosevelt from life during the time period mentioned. The results are shown on a Mint inaugural medal issued in 1933.

The medal depicts Roosevelt's profile facing right, not left as on the dime, but bears a similarity. Above all, it suggests that Sinnock had his own studies to draw upon in preparation of the dime and leads one to wonder why he would need to plagiarize another artist's work.

If, however, as Rochette contends, Burke's image of Roosevelt was widely known, it's not inconceivable that Sinnock arranged to have her drawing sent over for study. There's just no solid proof that he did. Letters from Roosevelt's relatives and others thanking Burke for her work on the dime are treasures and show that others support her claim, but cannot go far enough to fully substantiate it. The principals who could, including Ruth Wilson, have long since died.

This does not mean that her story should be ignored or dismissed. An accomplished artist and sculptor whose works have been and continue to be displayed at major art venues in the United States and elsewhere, Burke has no real need for additional credit. She's won numerous major art awards and has proven herself to herself and to the art world. At 94, she has no ax to grind, just a simple hope that someday people will recognize the design on the dime as hers.

Making up an elaborate story to promote herself as designer of the dime seems inconceivable, especially when you've met and gotten to know this charming, accomplished lady in person. Even if no one other than a few close associates and a numismatic writer here or there come to accept that she was responsible for the dime, she will always wholeheartedly believe it and will likely be content with that.

The door cannot be summarily closed on her story, but the passage of time has made it nearly impossible to jar it open. That she is a gifted sculptor, artist, and a remarkable woman cannot be denied. That her drawing of Roosevelt played a role in history is also without doubt. That it had a role in the dime's design will, however, likely always remain open to question.

Chapter 11

Initial controversy

Hoarding widespread as recall rumors plagued first issue of Lincoln cents

It sometimes seems as if nothing gets by the watchful eye of the American public. Other times you could parade an elephant down a major city street and not receive any notice, other than the disgruntled blare of a horn or two. It certainly must have seemed that way to Lincoln cent designer Victor D. Brenner, who raised more uproar than he bargained for when his initials, "V.D.B.," were placed on the reverse of the new Lincoln cent, released in 1909.

Unwanted initials

Although there was nothing new about a designer placing his initials on a coin he designed, Brenner's "V.D.B." would cause such a stir that rumors of a possible recall sprang up almost immediately. Today hardly a numismatist alive doesn't know that the 1909 San Francisco Mint issue with Brenner's initials on the reverse is valuable in all grades of preservation.

According to researcher Don Taxay, the decision to drop the initials from the coin can be traced to Treasury Secretary Franklin MacVeagh, who took exception to the appearance of Brenner's initials prominently positioned at the base of the coin's reverse. MacVeagh ordered suspension of coinage on Aug. 5, 1909, three

Treasury Secretary Franklin MacVeagh ordered a quick halt to coinage of the new Lincoln cent in 1909 due to the prominent placement of designer Victor D. Brenner's initials at the base of the reverse.

days after the official release. This despite the fact that he had approved use of the design earlier and ignoring the implications of the more than 28 million coins produced and distributed to subtreasuries and banks by the Philadelphia Mint, and nearly a half-million "V.D.B." cents from the San Francisco Mint. [1]

Mint engraver Charles E. Barber was ordered to place the initial "B" inconspicuously on the coin's reverse. Barber, however, favored removal of the initials from the hub. He argued that placement of a "B" on the coin might lead to confusion, as his initial, "B," appeared on the half dollar. More importantly, he didn't like the design and didn't want anyone to believe it had been prepared by his hand. [2]

Despite the protest raised over Brenner's initials on the cent, the practice of a placing an engraver's initials on a coin was not new. Christian Gobrecht, for example, placed "Gobrecht" on his silver dollars of 1836.

Brenner, of course, was hurt by the debate. The practice of putting the artist's or engraver's initials on coins goes back to ancient history. It was also well known, at least within numismatic circles.

In response to a reader's query in the December 1916 issue of Mehl's *Numismatic Monthly* about whether or not Brenner was ever imprisoned for placing his initials on the cent, B. Max Mehl wrote:

> "Why should he be? As far back as B.C. 400 we find the name of the engraver on the coins he designed. Take away from him this privilege and you deprive him of his most valued reward. The dollars of 1836 have 'C. GOBRECHT' on them, and the Lafayette-Washington dollars have 'Bartlett' in script at the base of the equestrian statue. The silver dollar coined from 1878 to 1904 has an 'M' on both obverse and reverse for the designer, George T. Morgan, the mint engraver. Our present type of silver coins have a 'B' on the bottom of the neck of Liberty, directly above the first figure of [the] date. This is the mark of Charles E. Barber, the mint's chief engraver. This 'B' is also found on the Columbian half-dollar." [3]

Brenner responds

In an Aug. 23, 1909, letter to American Numismatic Association President Farran Zerbe, Brenner told why he thought it was important to display an artist's initials on a coin. He wrote:

> "It is mighty hard for me to express my sentiments with reference to the initials on the cent. The name of the artist on a coin is essential for the student of history as it enables him to trace environments and conditions of the time said coin was produced. Much fume has been made about my initials as a means of advertisement; such is not the case. The very talk the initials has brought out has done more good for numismatics than it could do me personally.
>
> The cent not alone represents in part my art, but it represents *the type of art of our period.*
>
> The conventionalizing of the sheafs of wheat was done by me with much thought, and I feel that with the prescribed wording no better design could be obtained. The cent will wear out two of the last ones in time, due entirely to the hollow surface.

Brenner defended the appearance of his initials on the Lincoln cent, saying, "the name of the artist on a coin is essential for the student of history as it enables him to trace environments and conditions of the time" in which the coin was produced.

Original models for the cent placed "Brenner" in the position where "V.D.B." later appeared.

The original design had *Brenner* on it, and that was changed to the initials. Of course the issue rests with the numismatic bodies, and Europe will watch the outcome with interest." [4]

Meeting in Montreal in early August 1909, the ANA adopted a resolution protesting the removal of the Brenner's initials from the cent. Writing of the vote in his journal, Mehl said:

"The question of a designers' initials on a cent piece is not a vital one, and there is no doubt that the world is too little mindful of the artist's just claim to its recognition. But an artist who can design and execute a coin or medal of merit, certainly should have the privilege of attaching his name, or at least his initials, upon his work, the same as the painter places his name on the canvas and the sculptor on his work. St. Gaudens and Pratt, we believe, placed their names on the late issue of gold coins.

We should make concerted efforts to have the initials of Mr. Brenner retained on the Lincoln cents, not because Mr. Brenner is a member of the A.N.A. but for the historical knowledge it will convey to future generations.

The Lincoln cent is being admired by the public as an appreciative work of art; then why not retain the initials, which will keep up from being forgetful of the name of the artist whose genius conceived it." [5]

Speculation grows

News that the Mint was removing the initials lead to speculation that the coins would bring a premium. A run on subtreasuries and banks ensued.

The Sept.-Oct. 1909 issue of *The Numismatist* reported:

"About 25,000,000 had been coined and distributed to various sub-treasuries and banks throughout the country so that distribution could commence in all parts on the same day. As soon as it became known that a new coin had been issued places of distribution were besieged, particularly in New York, Boston, Philadelphia, Chicago and Saint Louis, where long lines formed leading to Sub-Treasuries, and continued each day with increased interest until August 5th, when the sign was displayed 'No More Lincoln Pennies.' " [6]

The quick halt to coinage of cents with the "V.D.B." initials led to the creation of one of the most famous 20th century U.S. coins — the 1909-S "V.D.B." It brings good premiums in all grades.

Limits were put on the number that could be had at any one time. Those who didn't want to wait in line were forced to pay a premium of two, three, or five cents.

"When no more were obtainable at Government supply places, stories in explanation were invented, 'going to be called in,' etc., and prices soared in different sections, as much as a dollar each being paid for specimens." [7]

Collier's Weekly ran a photograph of newspaper boys and messengers lined up on Aug. 4, 1909, in front of subtreasury building on New York's Wall Street. Limits, it said, had to be enforced on the number each received, as the newsboys were doing a "thriving business in them" — examples selling as high as 25 cents each.

Apparently the hobby was not yet aware of the scarce nature of the San Francisco issue with the "V.D.B." initials, as the Sept-Oct.

Brenner's initials were restored to the cent in 1918, appearing at the truncation of the Lincoln bust.

1909 issue of *The Numismatist* predicted:

> "Some day in the far distant future the numismatist may occasionally have to answer: 'Say, Mister, how much will you give me for one of those rare Lincoln cents made away back in 1909 when the United States were in America, — it's the rare kind with V.D.B. on it?' But to-day, and for untold days, so frequent will be the question that it seems advisable for the coin merchant to have in constant operation a phonograph that will grind out, 'No premium on Lincoln cents with V.D.B. on them, or with anything else on or off them.' " [8]

Despite this dire prediction, the 1909 "V.D.B." cent from San Francisco was immediately popular among collectors and remains one of the most sought-after 20th century coins. The "V.D.B." initials returned to the cent in 1918, positioned discreetly on the obverse at the truncation of the Lincoln figure, where no complaint could be raised and few would ever notice.

Chapter 12

Ice cream money

The tale of a little girl, a hot day, and a rare dime

One of the mysteries of U.S. coinage is the existence of the 1894-S dime, of which 24 were struck but less than 10 are known. The story behind this famous U.S. rarity is a mixture of fact and fiction that has so far defied explanation.

Uncertain origins

To this day collectors remain uncertain as to why only 24 dimes were struck at the San Francisco Mint in 1894. That 24 is the number of coins minted is affirmed by the Mint director's report for 1894, which lists $2.40 in dimes produced from Jan. 1 to June 30, 1894, the end of the fiscal year. [1]

The following year's report says 1,120,000 coins were minted during the fiscal year ending June 30, 1895. As this is the entire coinage recorded for 1895, no additional dimes were struck in 1894. But why?

Theories, of which there are several, have varied from a limited striking to balance the Mint's bullion accounts to production of two dozen dimes at the whim of the Mint director for distribution to his banker friends.

One of the first to try to shed light on the question was American Numismatic Association founder George F. Heath. In the June 1900 issue of *The Numismatist* Heath reported that collector J.C. Mitchel-

A great rarity, the 1894-S Barber dime remains steeped in mystery. Although mintage records indicate that 24 were struck, the exact reason for this small output is unknown.

son of Kansas City had "discovered an 1894-S dime." Mint authorities, Mitchelson said, informed him that though 24 were struck, only 14 went into circulation. The remaining 10 were restruck.[2] No reason was given why only 24 coins were struck or why the 14 remaining coins were released.

In the late 1920s prominent numismatist Farran Zerbe told a different tale, related to him in 1905 on a visit to the San Francisco Mint. Zerbe said:

> "To close a bullion account at the San Francisco Mint at the end of the fiscal year, June 30th, 1894, it was found necessary to show 40 cents, odd, in the year's coinage. The mint not having coined any dimes during the year, the dime dies were put to work, and to produce the needed 40 cents, 24 pieces were struck, any reasonable amount of even dollars over the 40 cents being readily absorbed in the account." [3]

Except for two or three coins saved as gifts, the remainder of the coinage, he said, went into a bag with other dimes and thereby entered circulation.

A rare treat

Today the most widely quoted theory is often ascribed to James G. Johnson, former "Clearing House" editor for *Coin World*. In the June 27, 1973, issue of *Coin World* Johnson told that he had been contacted by Guy L. Chapman of California, who explained that at a meeting of the Redwood Empire Coin Club in 1954 California dealer Earl Parker had placed two 1894-S dimes in his hand, offering the coins for sale.

Parker told Chapman that he had obtained the coins from Hallie Daggett, daughter of the former San Francisco Mint superintendent, John Daggett. John Daggett, upon learning that no dimes were to be struck in 1894 at the San Francisco Mint, agreed to mint some 1894-dated dimes for his banker friends. Three of these were given to Hallie with an admonishment from her father to keep the coins until she was as old as he was. This because he knew the coins would someday be valuable. However, on the way home from the mint, Hallie spent one of the coins on a dish of ice cream. [4]

The remainder of the 24 coins were distributed, three each, to seven bankers.

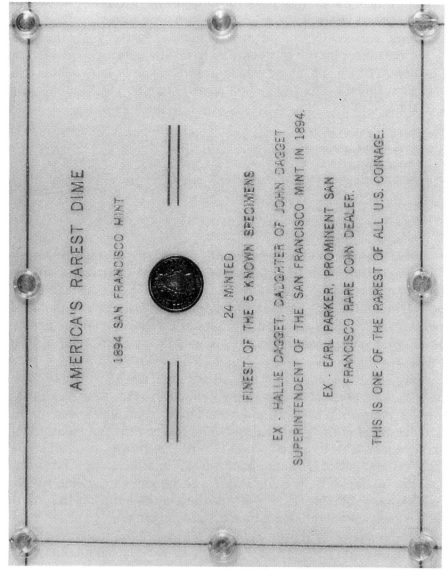

One of two 1894-S dimes dealer Earl Parker is said to have purchased in the early 1950s from Hallie Daggett, daughter of San Francisco Mint Director John Daggett. Today the number of known specimens is estimated to be nine.

Chapman told Johnson that he delayed making the purchase until he could consult with his wife that evening, but by next morning, Parker had already sold the coins.

Chapman's memory was at fault, at least in regard to the year in which he was supposedly offered the dimes. As William A. Burd notes in his article for the February 1994 issue of *The Numismatist*, Parker purchased his two specimens four years earlier, in 1950 — one of which then went to W.R. Johnson and the other sold as part of the January 1953 F.S. Guggenheimer Collection sale by Stack's of New York, where it was pedigreed to a relative of the mintmaster.

A slightly different story, which may be related to Parker's purchase, appeared in the February 1951 issue of *Numismatic Scrapbook Magazine*. A reader from San Francisco had forwarded a newspaper clipping telling of the sale of two specimens of the 1894-S dime and explaining that in 1894 a banker gave three dimes to his daughter and told her to save them, as the coins would some day be valuable. The magazine reported:

> "Recently the Ukiah [Calif.] woman sold two of them for $2,750.00 each. She looked high and low for the third specimen, but finally remembered that it was a hot day in 1894 when her father gave her those dimes and she visited an ice cream parlor on the way home.
>
> Now will the numismatist who laid out the $5,500.00 collaborate the story? ? ?" [5]

The story of Hallie Daggett and her squandering a part of her fortune on a dish of ice cream, whether true or a matter of fancy, has become an ingrained part of hobby folklore.

A forgotten dime

Playing off the popularity of the 1894-S dime, in 1992 the Professional Numismatists Guild, an organization of professional coin dealers, launched a promotion attempting to draw any additional specimens of the 1894-S dime and other U.S. rarities out of hiding. As part of its "Nationwide Search for a Million Dollars Worth of Missing Rare Coins," the PNG announced at the American Numismatic Association/PNG Early Spring Convention in Dallas in February 1992 that it was offering a reward for anyone finding a new specimen of the 1894-S dime and providing it to the organization for verification. Apparently hoping to avoid being deluged with 1894 dimes struck at

In 1992 the Professional Numismatics Guild launched a nationwide search for additional 1894-S dimes. PNG member Larry Whitlow explained that only those 1894 dimes bearing an "S" mintmark on the reverse were being sought. **Photo by the author.**

Philadelphia or New Orleans, the PNG stressed that only dimes for this year bearing an "S" mintmark were rare.

It offered free authentication to the first person to submit a genuine example and round-trip airline tickets to a major coin show, with hotel accommodations for three days and two nights, to whomever discovered one of the coins. A genuine example, valued at $250,000, was displayed for the press to see and photograph.

To date, the promotion has generated thousands of phone calls but no new examples. It did, however, bring one previously-known specimen out of hiding, the story of which was told by California dealer Ira Goldberg in "Silence of the 1894-S Dime — Subtitle: What a Dealer Won't Do for a Big Deal," in the July 7, 1992, issue of *Numis-*

matic News. Goldberg, a principal in Superior Stamp & Coin Co. Inc., said he had been contacted by a man from Chicago who had watched a Cable News Network report on the PNG search for missing 1894-S dimes. The man said it reminded him that he had purchased one these coins some years earlier. He now wanted to sell it.

The story was true. The man, later identified as John Deland, had obtained a genuine example nearly 20 years earlier from Bowers and Ruddy Galleries in Los Angeles, where it was being offered for $97,500. Amazingly, it was the only coin he ever purchased.

Deland walked into the gallery in 1974 looking to acquire either an 1804 silver dollar, a 1913 Liberty Head nickel, or an 1894-S dime — coins he had heard about as a youth. According to Goldberg, an 1804 dollar was available at the time for $125,000, but Deland opted for the less expensive coin.

Consigned to Superior's sale in August 1992 in Florida, his forgotten dime brought $165,000. [6]

Hallie's Comet

Probably the most bizarre result of the search came in the form of a 20-page typewritten letter postmarked from California submitted for publication to *Numismatic News*, signed simply, "Hallie's Comet." A shorter letter, along with a purported specimen of the 1894-S dime, was sent to the PNG so, as the writer explained, the dime could be conveyed to "some society or group which will see to its perpetual preservation and also its permanent display and accessibility to the public."

In the inventive March 27, 1994, letter, the writer said he decided to tell his story of his relationship with Hallie Daggett and the 1894-S dime at the urging of a collector friend. He included an 1848-dated letter he said was given to him by Hallie and a brass Green River Whiskey good-luck piece, crudely inscribed "HC" ("Haley's Comet"), for the person who would see that his 1848 letter found a proper home in a historical society.

The writer said he had carried his specimen of the 1894-S dime as a pocket piece for a number of years, after it had been given to him by his former girlfriend, Hallie Daggett, who had nicknamed him "Hallie's Comet." He said he met Hallie (apparently in 1901) while still a child living in San Francisco. Hallie, he said, regularly received coins from her father, the mint director.

"There came a day during all this coin-giving when Mr. Daggett handed Hallie a handful of gleaming new 1894 San Francisco mint dimes and told her that these particular dimes were not for spending but were a carefully selected portion of some small run of such dimes and that she should retain them as souvenirs through life," he wrote. "Hallie told me that she promised this, as any child will do, but that while she was indeed saving some of the dimes, she had already spent two of them, and one other one that she had not spent she was now giving to me.

"She said it was a special dime for her 'special beau'. She confessed to me having spent one dime on an ice cream float and having spent the other dime for a chicken tamale at the pushcart of a downtown corner vender, tamales being a rave gourmet treat with Hallie in those times.

"As for the 1894 dime she gave me, I soon pierced it and strung it about my neck, keeping it strictly out of sight, but when Hallie discovered this she politely demanded that I not carry the dime she had given me in such manner, to which demand I shortly acquiesced, whereupon I relegated the dime to my pocket as a good luck charm. I did not tell Hallie I still carried her dime about with me, as I was not sure whether or not she would approve my carrying the dime even in the well-hidden inner sanctum of my pocket."

The writer said he later lost his spot in her affections, but continued to carry the dime with him as a lucky piece. It was the only coin he ever collected in his life.

The letter rambles on through his service in World War I to his career in the Hollywood motion picture business, first as a cameraman in 1919 shooting "B" movies, including one silent flick with a youngster named Mickey McGuire, later known as Mickey Rooney, and still later on *Casablanca*, where he loaned his dime to a French girl who appears briefly in the film singing the French national anthem while playing an accordion. He says she carried the coin with her during these takes.

The writer also confesses to appearing as an extra in *Sunset Boulevard*, having been talked into taking the role by his friend Erich Von Stroheim, an early Hollywood director. According to Hallie's Comet, he can be spotted near the end of the film as one of the men "who stands on the stairway as Miss [Gloria] Swanson descends down the stairs, in a panning medium long shot." Before filming of this sequence started, he took a piece of electrician's tape and placed it on the back of his dime. He then affixed the dime to a large, ornate picture on the wall by a staircase, dedicating the coin's appearance in the film to Hallie.

"When the finished motion picture was released later on in 1950 I went to the theater and saw it, and when my own scene there on the stairway appeared I gandered not only myself but looked closely to see if I could make out the dime as Miss Swanson passed by it and surely enough it was there on the screen and could be made out, although slightly blurred by the panning maneuver of the camera."

He also told of the time he informed Magaret Hamilton, the Wicked Witch in *The Wizard of Oz*, of the story behind his rare dime. She wasn't much interested.

Additional portions of the letter tell, in detail, what type of child Hallie was and proclaim her to have been an accomplished musician, performing regularly at picnics for San Francisco Mint employees, including one he attended after Daggett's father had left the mint's employ.

"Mr. Daggett was most proud of Hallie's talents and encouraged her in many ways, including once buying her an expensive and professional-quality banjo, which Hallie became so proficient in using that she played it wonderfully, and sang wonderfully, at some of the grand picnics the employees of the San Francisco mint used to throw during Mr. Daggett's tenure as head of that mint. Hallie got up boldly before the crowd and firing up tonsils and banjo laid into 'Green Grow the Lilacs' like I never heard before or since. The cheers of the crowd were loud enough to start a quake, which perhaps is how the 1906 Frisco earth-dance commenced. Come to think, this may have been after Mr. Daggett left his position as mint head, but he was there at the picnics always, and I believe did cheer louder for Hallie's entertaining ways than almost anyone there, save for myself."

Much of the remainder of the letter, said to have been written over a period of time, is devoted to the writer's work in Hollywood, who the best actors are and were, his love for and thoughts of Hallie, her later life, and how, even though having passed his 100th birthday some years prior, he was still actively working on films up until shortly before sending the coin to Paul Koppenhaver, then PNG executive director.

At one point in the narrative he tells that he noticed he had inadvertently sent Koppenhaver the wrong coin. He corrected the oversight, locating the dime in his button jar. After cleaning it, "making it nice and shiny," he examined the coin with a powerful reading glass to be certain that the date was indeed 1894 and that it carried the "S" mintmark. His nephew then forwarded the dime to Koppenhaver.

Alas, though, despite his best efforts to gain fame for his relation to the 1894-S dime and Hallie Daggett, the passage of time weighs against him and his creative story. According to Burd's research, Hallie Daggett would have been 22 years old in 1901, the year Hallie's Comet claims to have first been associated with the dime. Despite having admitted to having passed his 100th birthday some years back, to have been Hallie's boyfriend he would have to have been considerably older, pushing 110 to 115.

There was one other slight problem. Well, maybe it's not so slight. When the coin arrived at Koppenhaver's office it was heavily worn, as might be expected of a pocket piece, but the hole Hallie's Comet said he put through the coin was directly through the date!

Chapter 13

'Twisted Tails'

Thoughts, outcries, misconceptions and other interesting tidbits about U.S. coins

From delightful tales of foreign intrigue, chicanery, myths and misunderstandings to famed collectors and their coins, the historical account of numismatics from the U.S. side of the ledger is blotted with interesting facts and fancies for the collector to explore and enjoy.

As is often the case with the written word, facts can become distorted or bent out of shape. Passage of time will warp reality, allowing baseless rumors to flourish, ill-skewed facts to be repeated, and even bald-faced lies to be accepted as truth. As if following Mark Twain's advice, "get your facts first, and then you can distort them as much as you please," there is a passion by some to accept a good story over the truth any day.

Numismatics, as the prior chapters have shown, is not immune. In fact, it's a hotbed for "good" stories.

What follows are just a few of the more delightful, a few of the better known, and a few that hark to the evolution of the hobby and its ever-expanding base of knowledge. Beginning with the popular "Orphan Annie" dime and ending with the "Value You Me as You Please" Higley copper, it's by no means intended to be a complete listing, rather a random sampling to whet the appetite.

An orphaned coin

Replete with its own colorful moniker, the 1844 dime may not be scarcest Seated Liberty dime but it's certainly one of the most fabled, carrying with it an enchanting story of Mexican senoritas, lovesick soldiers and shiny bangles made of dimes.

Despite being scarce only in higher grades, the 1844 dime, with a mintage of 72,500, continues to attract attention, bringing good premiums in all grades. This is probably because of the promotional efforts of Frank C. Ross, a writer from the Kansas City area, who some believe provided the coin with the nickname, "Orphan Annie," by which it is known today. [1]

Whether or not Ross was responsible for tagging the coin "Orphan Annie," it is certain that he presented one of the most vivid accounts of a once popular rumor of how this dime came to be scarce. In a 1946 *Numismatic Scrapbook Magazine* article, Ross said that numismatists had been searching for years for the reason why 1844 dimes are rare. One of the most popular stories to emerge, he said, was that the coins went with the U.S. Army to Mexico, where the dimes were used to win sexual favors from Mexican senoritas. [2] The story went something like this . . .

In 1844, with a surplus of dimes on hand, the new sacked and counted 1844 dimes were placed in the corner of a Philadelphia Mint vault for future use. As dimes were needed, the coins were taken from rows at the front of the vault, thereby leaving the 1844 dimes undisturbed.

This probably would have remained the case if troops hadn't been mustered for an invasion of Mexico. The expedition's paymaster made requisition for a large supply of small change to be used by the soldiers. Thus, the 1844 dimes, conveniently bagged and counted, went with the soldiers to Mexico.

Once in Mexico's capital, the soldiers became homesick and longed for female companionship. It was then that one of their number came upon a plan to attract the local senoritas. Noticing that they liked to wear fancy bangles, he fashioned some bracelets using the 1844 dimes.

It worked. A booming enterprise followed as others in his company stumbled over each other, lining up to buy the bracelets. Not an 1844 dime escaped the love-crazed surge. When the soldiers came home, the bracelets stayed behind with their new loves. But, like time, love is often fleeting. The soldiers were soon forgotten and the bracelets melted, the silver being reminted into Mexican coins.

This was just one of many legends developed by playful, overactive minds concerning the scarcity of 1844 dimes. Other equally ambitious tales were:

— That the coins were improperly alloyed, so most of the mintage was melted at the Mint.

— The entire issue had been bought up by a speculator, few survived.

— A bank in New Orleans requisitioned Washington for $5,000 in dimes.

— Fifty-thousand were shipped by boat but lost in a storm.

— The coins were lost in the Great Chicago Fire.

— The dimes gravitated to Pennsylvania and were swept away in the Great Johnstown Flood.

— Seventy thousand of the coins were sent overland to the forty-niners in California via the Santa Fee Trail. Along the way, the coins were seized by bandits who hid the loot. The bandits were later killed, taking knowledge of the secret hiding place with them for eternity to their graves.[3]

Missing flag

Where's the missing flag? When the Jefferson nickel was released in 1938 a rumor spread quickly that the depiction of the White House on the coin's reverse was missing the U.S. flag. The coins would, no doubt, be recalled. The rush to obtain Jefferson nickels was on.

Problem was, the building is Monticello, Thomas Jefferson's home, not the White House.

The rumor apparently started after the winning designs were released to the press, and was circulated by a prominent radio commentator.

This wasn't the only rumor linked to the Jefferson nickel's release, another claimed that the coins were too wide to fit into subway slots and were being recalled.

Seeing red

Tales of subversive acts by foreign powers and attempts to impress their ideologies on Americans are certainly not new in this country. It's probably not that surprising then that those who revel in defending the United States against unseen enemies would scrutinize U.S. coins for evidence of foreign intrigue.

One of the best-known rumors about Communists infiltrating the U.S. Mint is that the initials "JS" on the Roosevelt dime, issued in 1946, stood for Joseph Stalin. So pervasive was this story that Mint Director Nellie Tayloe Ross found it necessary to publicly refute the claim, explaining that the initials belonged to Mint engraver John Sinnock.

Certain ambitious versions of this bit of nonsense add that President Franklin D. Roosevelt had promised to place Stalin's initials on the coin when he met with the communist ruler at the Yalta Conference in February 1945. This assuming that Roosevelt knew his portrait would appear on the dime after his death! He didn't.

Lurking comrade

The same basic rumor — that the "JRS" initials represented Joseph Stalin — also plagued the release of the Franklin half dollar in 1948. The half dollar was designed by Sinnock.

One version of this story charged that it was a communist lurking in the Mint who secretly placed his comrade's initials on the coin. [4]

Hammer and sickle

Don't forget the Kennedy half dollar. Some fell for the story that the stylized initials "GR," for Mint engraver Gilroy Roberts, were the work of another runaway Communist, bent on showing his country's hammer and sickle on a U.S. coin.

Entry wound

If it weren't bad enough that Gilroy Roberts' initials on the Kennedy half dollar were touted as Russia's hammer and sickle, others morbidly proclaimed that the location of the initials — at the truncation of the bust of Kennedy — marked the point at which one of Lee Harvey Oswald's bullets struck the president.

Our fascist dime

Lesser known from the rumor mill, but basically on the same level as the communist-infiltration tales, was the Mercury dime's supposed link to fascism. Even though the fasces (a Roman symbol of authority) were incorporated into Adolph Weinman's design long before the rise of fascism, the Mercury dime engendered criticism for its supposed reference to the hated ideology and Italy's ruler, Benito Mussolini.

Under the headline "He'll Find it There, All Right" the April 1926 issue of *The Numismatist* quotes from the *Chicago Evening Post* that:

Despite being released long before World War II, many came to believe that the reverse design for Adolph Weinman's Winged Liberty dime showed a design linked to fascism.

"Anyone who denounces Mussolini for the adoption of a battle-ax as the symbol of the Fascisti, says Representative Sol Bloomsays, better take a look at a dime.

Even if the fasces were adopted long before the rise of fascism, some argued that future generations might get the wrong idea of the offending symbol was left on U.S. coins." [5]

In 1936, a letter sent by J. Milton Strauses (a member of the American Numismatic Association and the California Coin Club) to Andrew L. Somers, chairman of the House Committee on Coinage, Weights and Measures, urged:

"The fasces, which is the emblem of Fascism, the present form of government in Italy, strangely enough appears on the reverse of our dime. Although it appears on this coinage as early as 1916, and although it was not officially adopted by Mussolini and his followers until 1919, future world historians delving into the past through numismatics, as is often their custom, are liable to draw the conclusion that the United States and not Italy was the birthplace of Fascism.

Let us somehow immediately correct any such possibility, and at least remove this design, as the fasces is now most un-American and might some day cast a reflection on our constitutional form of government." [6]

Old battle ax

The Mercury dime's fasces were also a source of sarcasm. When the coin was released in 1916 some termed it the "golf coin" because of the resemblance of the fasces to a golf club. Others called it the "battle ax" dime.

Watchful waiting

Designer Adolph Weinman's initials, "AW," on the Mercury dime's obverse, which were mistaken by some to be a single "W," set people to wondering if the initial stood for then-President Woodrow Wilson. Or, with the escalating concerns of war in Europe, "watchful waiting." [7]

Dime recall

Usually it's the general public who first grasps and spreads coinage recall rumors. Not so with the release of the Mercury dime in 1916.

Numismatists in New Orleans advised collectors that placement of designer Adolph Weinman's initials on the coin's obverse violated "the edict which prohibits advertising on the currency of the country," and would soon lead to a recall. Collectors, they said, should save the new coins for "they would likely soon sell at a premium."

Mehl's Numismatic Monthly for January 1917 advised likewise:

"It will be remembered that when the Lincoln penny first was introduced, the designer of that coin was discovered to have labeled the piece with his initials. The treasury did its best to recall the pennies of the type in circulation and new dies were made with the initials eliminated. The same system may be adopted in the case of the new dimes, a press dispatch from Washington says, though $2,850,000 of the new dimes have been coined." [8]

No recall was ever forthcoming. If collectors had looked closely at the reverse of the new Walking Liberty half dollar, also by Weinman, they would have found his initials located on that coin as well, under the tip of the eagle's left wing feathers.

Mock-up

1964 Peace dollar?

There is no doubt that more than 300,000 Peace dollars were struck bearing a 1964 date. What is in doubt is whether any survived.

In August 1964 President Lyndon Baines Johnson authorized a return to the coinage of silver dollars, which had ended nearly 30 years earlier. The new coins were to use Anthony De Francisci's "Peace" design from the silver dollar issued from 1921-1935.

The act authorized coinage of 45 million, of which, 316,076 were struck at the Denver Mint before congressional bickering and collector protest led to an order in May 1965 to halt coinage.

Although the Mint firmly maintains that all 1964 Peace dollars were melted, and that none were released into circulation, unverified rumors still exist that a few specimens survived the melting pot.

1964 Franklin?

Also rumored is the existence of 1964-dated Franklin half dollars. The design was changed in that year in honor of the nation's fallen leader, John F. Kennedy.

Despite denials by the Mint and the coin's engraver, John Sinnock, rumors persist that at least one specimen of the Franklin design escaped the Mint bearing the 1964 date.

Fat mistress

When Mint engraver John Reich's Capped Bust design for the nation's coinage began appearing on half dollars and $5 gold half eagles in 1807 baseless rumors spread that the artist had portrayed his "fat mistress" on the coins. Reich's robust Liberty later appeared on U.S. dimes and quarters as well.

Weighty proposal

Tradition holds that John Hull of Boston became so wealthy from his issuance of Colonial Pine Tree shillings that when it came time for his daughter, Hannah, to marry Samuel Sewall, her marriage

dowry was made up of her weight in freshly minted silver Pine Tree shillings, or about 500 British pounds, a considerable sum in those days.

Her husband later became a judge, presiding over Salem witchcraft trials, where he condemned 19 people to their deaths.

Witch pieces

During the heyday of the witch trials in Salem, Mass., superstition held that if you carried a bent silver coin in your pocket it would ward off witches. This, some say, may account for bent examples of early Massachusetts Colonial coinage.

If it is true, it's likely Judge Sewall found ready use for his wife's rumored dowry of Pine Tree shillings.

Africa bound

If it's rare, it must have been lost at sea. The 1799 large cent was not spared such rumors, one of which claimed that the coins sank with a ship bound from Salem, Mass., to the coast of Africa.

How do you say . . .?

Some people get all wound up over the proper and improper use of words and terminology. Others don't really care. Numismatists, as a whole, likely fall into the former category. Just call a U.S. cent a penny, even in casual conversation, and watch the fur fly.

Numismatists are a proud bunch — especially when it comes to their specialized knowledge.

Question: Is it more accurately described as an Indian Head nickel or a Buffalo nickel? Is it a Mercury dime or a Winged Liberty dime?

How about Christian Gobrecht's famous Liberty for the coins of mid-1800s? Are the coins better described as Seated Liberty or Liberty Seated?

Get on the wrong side of any of these and you're likely to raise a long-winded debate as to what history shows as the proper usage.

This trait is nothing new to collectors of U.S. coins. For example, collectors were quick to point out that the buffalo on the 1913-1938 nickel is more accurately termed a bison (yet they continue to call the coin a Buffalo nickel).

They take pride in telling that the figure on the obverse of Adolph Weinman's dime is not really that of the Roman god Mercury. Rather, it's Liberty with wings attached to her cap. The wings symbolize "liberty of thought."

Then there's the fact that there is three times as much copper in the U.S. five-cent piece than nickel, yet the public persists in calling the coin a nickel. Actually, most would probably be surprised to know that, because of its nickel content, the first Flying Eagle cents were called nickels in their day. [9] That is, when they weren't being referred to as "buzzard cents."

There's nothing real wrong with all this. It's part of the fun of the hobby.

Back in the early 1900s it was common for dimes, quarters and half dollars to be called "Morgans." This carried over to later coin albums, which spread the incorrect usage.

Any numismatist worth his salt knows that George T. Morgan designed the dollar, 1878-1921, not the dime, 1892-1916, quarter, 1892-1916, and half dollar, 1892-1915. Those coins were by Charles E. Barber and are correctly known today as Barber dimes, quarters and half dollars. Yet there are probably some old-time numismatists out there still calling these coins Morgans.

Sit pretty

Just as the story goes that George and Martha Washington provided silver plate for the nation's first coinage, so it is said that Martha Washington posed for the design on the 1792 half disme. It's a tradition pretty well disputed today but one of those romantic tales many probably wish were true.

Disarming belief

The Peace dollar, issued from 1921-1935, was a prime target for criticism and misconception. Its story is well documented in the pages of *The Numismatist*, as are the outcries from the general press which are captured in February and March 1922 issues of the American Numismatic Association's journal.

ANA President Farran Zerbe first proposed the coin to mark the end of World War I and restoration of peace. News that the early designs for the new coin included one showing a broken sword led to the mistaken belief that the coin had been inspired by the Conference on the Limitation of Armaments being held at that time in Washington, D.C.

The *New York Herald*, for example, said that although a new silver dollar symbolic of an era of peace was a good idea, in attempting to portray the idea behind the disarmaments conference, the artist showed an eagle standing on a broken sword — the symbol either of surrender, a battle lost, or that the sword's owner had disgraced himself.

"But America has not broken its sword," the *Herald* challenged. "It has not been cashiered or beaten; it has not lost allegiance to itself. The blade is bright and keen and wholly dependable." [10]

Line's bizzay!

Others thought the Peace dollar's obverse, modeled after the Anthony De Francisci's wife, Theresa, made Liberty look like one of that era's flappers. They termed the coin the "flapper dollar."

The *Wall Street Journal* quipped: "If words were issuing from her lips they would hardly take the more elegant languor of 'Line's bizzay!' They would more probably be, 'Say, lissen!' " [11]

The paper called for the coin's redesign, saying, "the whole thing is bad." It suggested the Peace dollar be withdrawn from circulation and a new design commissioned through a nationwide competition.

"It's not too much to hope that we can at least evolve something

The Peace dollar was subject to a lot of criticism when it was released. Some thought the design too weak — not portraying the nation's determination to defend itself.

artistically above the level of the magazine cover," the *Journal* lamented. [12]

Doesn't stack up

Besides criticism of the design, others attacked the new Peace dollar for its inability to stack properly, trotting out the age-old fear that the coins would be recalled. A Feb. 2, 1922, press dispatch from New York reported:

> "Future financiers, now operating as messenger boys in Wall street, have started a drive to corner the newly coined 'Peace' silver dollar, it was learned today. The coin, of which slightly more than a million were minted, are selling at a premium of twenty-five to fifty cents each — the youthful buyers playing a 'hunch' that the issue will be recalled because of criticism of its design and its general make-up, which does not admit of easy stacking." [13]

Mint Director Raymond T. Baker was left to calm fears with an announcement that the coins would not be withdrawn. Baker scolded that "designs for dollars or any other form of currency are not made up to suit the arbitrary whims of the Director." Rather, the designs were submitted to eight leading sculptors and passed by a committee of artists. [14]

Fast running coward

Eagles have been under assault for a number of years, not only in nature, but in the nature of how they are portrayed on U.S. coins. Just about every time a new coin has been issued, someone has complained about its eagle. From the scrawny eagle found on the first 1792 half dismes and 1794 dollars to modern U.S. coinage, the cry of foul has arisen.

Some of the complaints have been totally erroneous, others just plain silly. Take for example a 1925 press dispatch from New York in which Harmon Pumpelly Read of Albany criticized the eagle on the new Standing Liberty quarter.

Using a 1904 Barber quarter and a 1920 Standing Liberty quarter as props, he argued that the new eagle broke the rules of heraldry. Read said:

> "On the old coin the eagle is in an upright position with wings extended, conveying the symbol of power and empire. The eagle is facing forward — that is bravery. The eagle on the new coin is not an American eagle. It is facing in the wrong direction. No power and emphasis here. That bird signifies cowardice. The fact that it is winging across the coin symbolizes speed, I suppose. A coward, and a fast running one." [15]

Tar and feathers

Another eagle lambasted for its lack of proper dignity was that by Adolph Weinman for the reverse of Walking Liberty half dollar.

Ornithologist Frank Chapman, charged that "the artist has made this bird a terrestrial fowl, striding or marching on the ground like a turkey-cock, and with as much dignity as one." Another critic lampooned the the eagle's attire, saying, "the eagle looks as though it were wearing overalls and marching through hot tar." [16]

Hot toes

From hot tar to hot toes — the eagle side of Weinman's half dollar didn't garner all of the barbs. Of the obverse and its depiction of a rather large sun in the background, one observer cautioned, "Liberty in sandals taking giant strides across the face might burn her toes, if she should step one millimeter nearer the rising sun." [17]

Sicklied over

In 1942 the *Chicago Daily News*, then owned by Secretary of the Navy Frank Knox, took exception to the nation's coinage as being, well . . . too wimpy. In a June 16 editorial, the paper groused about a trend toward pacifist coins it said began in 1916 with the release of new dimes, quarters and halves. It charged:

> "The result has been a set of pacifist coins all sicklied over with peace at any price, except the Lincoln penny and the Buffalo nickel which survived the pacifist craze. The Jefferson nickel recently issued is also immune, altho the obverse with its mechanical-looking image of Monticello makes it resemble some of those pre-war beer checks." [18]

The *News* also disliked the Washington quarter for its arrowless eagle perched on a fasces and loathed the eagle on the Standing Liberty quarter because it carried nothing in its claws. The Walking Liberty half dollar was also at fault because of its "undefiant" eagle with folded wings.

Probably the most offensive, however, was the Peace dollar, of which the *News* satirized:

"When the new dollar appeared, it was something! The wellfed classic girl with her tasteful coiffure of wheat and cotton had been replaced by a gal with adenoids who hadn't been to a beauty parlor in months. She was supposed to be 'Peace,' but didn't look much like it.

The eagle on the other side looked suspiciously like a tom turkey. He was on a pedestal of peace with plenty of olive foliage but nothing to fight with but his talons and beak, and they didn't look very terrible. One commentator at the time remarked that 'no little lamb will flee to the fold when the shadow of that bird falls across the valley.' " [19]

Coins have been considered keys to history, the paper explained, historians of the future looking back on these disarmed eagles would be justified in assuming that there was peace throughout this period.

"Give those arrows back to the American eagle and make our money tell the truth!" it pleaded. [20]

Valuable cornerstone

Records indicate that one 1870-S $3 gold coin was struck for inclusion in the cornerstone of the San Francisco Mint building. Yet, in 1911, a genuine 1870-S $3 gold coin appeared for sale in an offering by dealer William Woodin.

Some speculate it's a duplicate and that an additional example remains secreted among the relics within the Old Mint's cornerstone. Others believe the Woodin sale piece is the only example. No one knows for certain.

Light up

A note from an "S.T., Chicago" in the May 1945 issue of *The Numismatist* reports on the discovery of an unusual 1944 Lincoln head cent.

S.T. said of the coin, "With a strong magnifier I can see the faint outline of a cigarette in Lincoln's mouth." S.T. was obviously having more basic problems, as he also wrote, "If you want to please a lot of us collectors, you should print the 'Reports of Club Meetings' in a much larger type. They give me a lot of trouble." [21]

The editor suggested he get new glasses.

Weak link

Placement of a design of linked rings (likely representing the unity of the Colonies as a new nation) on the reverse of the first coinage of large cents in 1793 was deemed improper. It was termed by one newspaper as a "bad omen of liberty." The design was quickly replaced.

Is there a second example of the 1870-S $3 gold coin in the corner-stone of the Old San Francisco Mint? No one knows for certain.

Two-headed monster

Two-headed or two-tailed coins are not new to the hobby, although those who make their living answering questions from the general public constantly field questions from those who think they've struck it rich through the acquisition of such oddities. Known as "magician" pieces, and by other names, all such two-headed coins are pure fabrications, which give way to their alteration upon close examination with a magnifying glass.

Still, even when faced with this standard, tried-and-true explanation, some people just don't get the message. The October-December 1931 issue of *The Numismatist* recorded a wave of reports of two-headed coins were appearing in newspapers, including one collector who was so adamant that his coin was real that he wanted $5,000 for his specimen, saying it was unlikely anyone could find another such piece, even if they offered $100,000! [22]

Genuine

Fake

Nickel epidemic

Since the hobby first learned of the existence of five 1913 Liberty Head nickels there have been rumors of a missing sixth example. The hobby got more than it bargained for, however, when rewards from Texas dealer B. Max Mehl and the eccentric Col. E.H.R. Green began appearing in the 1930s. No additional genuine examples were found, however, fakes began popping up all over the place.

Stars and bars

First issues of the Shield nickel, released just after the end of the Civil War, displayed rays between the stars on the reverse. Some saw these "stars and bars" as representative of the Confederate battle flag — put there, they believed, to promote the defeated Southern cause. [23]

Josh's golden racket

Soon after the release of the Liberty Head nickel, in 1883, rumors began to circulate that the coins, which displayed the "V" for "five cents" on the reverse without the addition of word "cents," would be recalled. It was also reported that the coins were being plated and passed off as $5 gold coins.

According to numismatic lore, the leader among all of these petty crooks was Josh Tatum, a deaf-mute from Boston who took $50 worth of the new coins to a Boston pawnbroker owning a gold-plating machine to be plated. Tatum then set out to spend one of his new "gold" coins at a tobacco store, where he purchased a five-cent cigar by laying the coin on the counter and receiving $4.95 in change. He repeated this process at various tobacco stores, disposing of the entire 1,000 coins within a week.

Tatum and the jeweler decided to plate 5,000 more and took their scam on the road between Boston and New York, dumping about

2,000 more before authorities caught up with them.

At his trial, the defense presented by Tatum's lawyer was simple: Josh never asked for change.

The case being dismissed, the government moved to stop any further abuse by placing the word "cents" on the coin. [24]

Real Racketeers

Some collectors have come to believe that "original" plated Racketeer nickels — those made up in the 1800s to pass as $5 gold coins — can be distinguished from later alterations by the presence or lack of a reeded edge. This, of course, ignores the possibility that modern plated versions could also be reeded.

In 1960 a collector warned readers of *Numismatic Scrapbook Magazine* that Racketeer nickels of his day were strictly phoney. Modern con men don't take the trouble to reed the edge, he said. Rather, they buy 1883 "no cents" nickels at 35 cents each, plated the coins with five cents worth of gold and sell the "new" Racketeer nickels to suckers at $2 to $5 each.

"I believe that he makes the old time crooks look like real pikers," he said of the modern fakers. [25]

Who's joshing who?

Another favorite story among numismatists is that the popular phrase of disbelief "you're joshing" originated with Josh Tatum and his passing of plated $5 gold coins. Sorry, as writer Eric von Klinger pointed out, its origin dates to much earlier.

The *American Thesaurus of Slang*, for example, notes of "josh": "To banter, 'kid' (U.S.-1845). Origin obscure. The earliness of the usage rules out the supposition that it derives from 'Josh Billings,' who had not yet gained a reputation as a humorist." [26] So it does with Josh Tatum.

Mintmark goes

Coinage shortages during the mid-1960s led to a search for solutions and scapegoats. Thus, in 1965, mintmarks were removed from U.S. coins, this in the erroneous belief that hoarding by collectors was part of the problem. With protest from collectors, mintmarks were restored to U.S. coins in 1968.

Wrong 'O'

When the Franklin half dollar was released in 1948 rumors sprang up, as they had with the dime, that Sinnock's initials on the half dollar represented Joseph Stalin. The coin's reverse also created a stir when it was rumored that the placement of a small "o" in the word

"of" in "United States of America" had been a mistake and the coins would be recalled. The same story circulated for the Memorial reverse of the Lincoln cent upon its release in 1959.

Withdrawal woes

When the announcement came that the San Francisco Mint was closing its doors in 1955, the rumor mills were ripe. Half dollars, dimes, and cents, the only coins struck for circulation that year bearing the "S" mintmark, were hoarded in the wake of tales of yet another recall.

Germ ridden

One of the most interesting U.S. coin designs is the sunken design by Bela Lyon Pratt for the gold $2.50 and $5 coins, issued beginning

in 1908. Soon after its release, complaints were aired that the coin was a ready receptacle for dirt and would possibly help transmit disease.

Despite these concerns, Pratt's coins continued to be minted through 1929 and were no more the cause of health worries than other coins.

Free F.O.R.D.

A bizarre rumor circulating prior to World War I claimed that a person finding four U.S. dimes with the mintmarks F, O, R, and D would win a car from the Ford Motor Co. The story made its rounds through the general press, with one New York newspaper, the *Utica Herald Dispatch*, forced to explain:

> "Because of the offer of a prize some firm is said to have made to any person who shall combine four different mint mark letters on 10-cent silver pieces, so as to spell a certain word of four letters, many Uticans are searching for the four coins that are said to bear these letters. Their search is hopeless. Two of the letters are 'F' and 'R.' There is no coin ever struck that bears either of these letters as a mint mark." [27]

The article went on to name the various mints and their mintmarks — Philadelphia (no mintmark), Charlotte (C), Carson City (CC), Dahlonega (D), San Francisco (S), New Orleans (O) and Denver (D) — to prove that it couldn't be done.

It added, however, that "the combination would-be prize winners are searching for can easily be formed from the legend 'United

States of America' on the dimes" and other coins of the United States. [28]

Happy motoring

To assist the war effort, the Mint changed from a copper composition for the cent to a zinc-coated steel version for one year, in 1943. A few examples are known to have escaped the Mint struck on copper planchets.

Rumors circulated in the 1940s that the Ford Motor Co. would give a car to anyone finding a 1943 copper cent. It wasn't true, but it probably led to the creation of additional bogus copper-plated cents of that year.

'D-less' cent

Among U. S. cents one of the dates, actually mintmarks — or perhaps more appropriately, a coin without a mintmark — that has caused the biggest row is the 1922 "plain" cent. Even today controversy remains as to how much if any of the "D" for "Denver" can show on the cent for it qualify as a high-premium coin.

As no cents were struck in 1922 at the Philadelphia Mint, theories were quickly developed as to how the "D-less" cents could have come into being. These ranged from the work of an unscrupulous mint employee to the mintmark having been left off the master die by mistake.

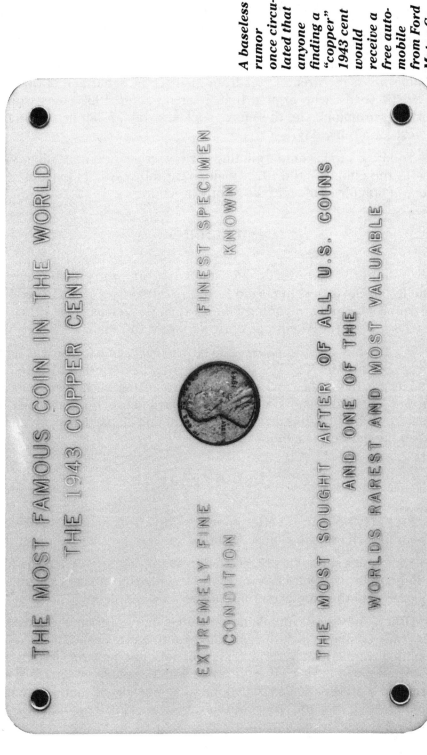

THE MOST FAMOUS COIN IN THE WORLD

THE 1943 COPPER CENT

FINEST SPECIMEN

KNOWN

EXTREMELY FINE

CONDITION

THE MOST SOUGHT AFTER OF ALL U.S. COINS

AND ONE OF THE

WORLDS RAREST AND MOST VALUABLE

A baseless rumor once circulated that anyone finding a "copper" 1943 cent would receive a free automobile from Ford Motor Co.

217

But, as the *Empire Investors Report* once noted, "No amount of wishful thinking will make a 1922 'plain' cent a 1922 'Philadelphia' cent." [29] The coin was the product of a clogged Denver Mint die.

One determined collector didn't care. The July 1937 issue of *The Numismatist* records a letter from Maurice D. Scharlack of Corpus Christi, Texas, who argued that, D or no D, *all* 1922 coins would bring a premium. He, therefore, socked away 25,000 in a wooden chest for a rainy day. [30]

Today, a similar minor minting variety would add only slight value to the coin. For the 1922 "plain" cent, however, its place in the lore of Lincoln cents and the hobby is secure.

Shy model

Up until the early 1970s numismatists were pretty well in agreement that Doris Doscher, a model from Whitson, N.Y., had posed for Hermon MacNeil's Standing Liberty quarter, released in 1916. As early as 1917 *The Numismatist* had reported the same.

In 1972, however, Irene MacDowell, then 92, came forward as having posed for MacNeil. MacDowell was the wife of Hermon MacNeil's tennis partner and a close family friend. MacDowell claimed to have posed for the design for a period of 10 days before her husband objected. A decision, it is said, was made among all parties involved to keep her service as a model a secret. [31]

Oh the agony!

Probably no coin is better known today for its general dislike by the public than the Susan B. Anthony dollar.

Sometimes sarcastically referred to as the "Agony" dollar, the Anthony dollar is often criticized for its similarity in size to the U.S. quarter and the confusion this causes.

Others, however, complain that coin is ugly, condemning designer Frank Gasparro for the depiction of suffragette Susan B. Anthony on its obverse. It's an unfair criticism, not only because Gasparro's rejected Flowing Hair Liberty design would have been far more attractive than the coin as issued, but also because it's a misconception. Like it or not, the coin bears a striking resemblance to Anthony.

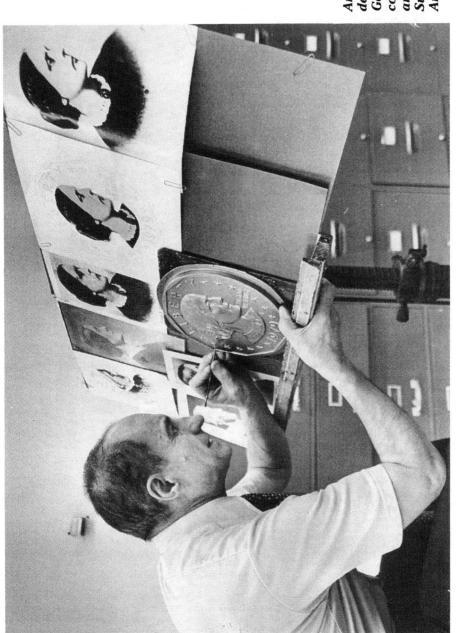

Anthony dollar designer Frank Gasparro with coinage models and portraits of Susan B. Anthony.

Rum soaked

One of the more interesting pieces within the U.S. Colonial series is an issue of copper tokens dated 1737 and 1739, known to collectors as Higley coppers. The first of these pure copper issues bore the legend "Value of Three Pence," but protests from the community eventually caused issuer John Higley to retain the Roman numeral III, but change the inscription to read "Value Me as You Please."

Tradition has it that Higley, an ingenious blacksmith with a taste for rum, made up the coins to support his drinking habit. Rum, you see, was threepence a glass in those days.

Endnotes

Chapter 1: What's in a name

1. Although the traditionally quoted number of "missing" models is one, Fraser wrote in an undated letter to George E. Roberts, Mint director (1889-1907, 1910-1914), that: "Before the nickel was made I had done several portraits of Indians, among these Iron Tail, Two Moons and one or *two* [italics added] others, and probably got characteristics from those men in the heads on the coins, but my purpose was not to make a portrait but a type."
2. W. H. De Shon, "The New Five-Cent Piece," *The Numismatist*, May 1913, p. 239.
3. "The New Five Cent Piece," *The Numismatist*, March 1913, p. 130.
4. Undated letter from Fraser to Roberts, supplied to Charles Bevard by the Treasury Department in response to an Aug. 3, 1988, letter from Bevard asking for information on the models for the Indian Head nickel.
5. See, for example, Elmo Scott Watson (titled through use of photos) "From Now on You'll be Seeing [Monticello and Jefferson] on Your Nickels, in Place of [Indian and bison]," Shelby, Mich. *Oceana Herald*, 4 March 1938.
6. Interview with Bevard, 1990.
7. Ibid.
8. Ibid.
9. Marianne F. Miller, "Buffaloed by the Buffalo Nickel," *Numismatic Scrapbook Magazine*, October 1956, p. 1697.
10. Ibid., p. 1703.
11. Ibid.
12. Leonard J. Ratzman, "The Buffalo Nickel, A 50-Year-Old Mystery," *Whitman Numismatic Journal*, June 1964, p. 27.
13. "The Head on the Current Nickel," *The Numismatist*, July 1931, p. 485.
14. Ratzman, p. 28.
15. Ibid., p. 29.
16. Ibid., p. 31. The obituary notice circulated by the Associated Press at the time of the chief's death in 1967 states that John Big Tree once told a correspondent that he received $1.50 an hour

for a three-hour sitting for Fraser.

17. See " 'The Most Famous Coin' Famous Buffalo Nickel Only One of James E. Fraser's Great Works," *Coin World*, 23 December 1964, pp. 48, 54, 70. Reprint of article from Spring 1957 issue of *News From the Front*, a publication of the Home Insurance Co., New York, N.Y., edited by Kenneth Dunshee.

18. Alice Glaser, "The Indian-Head Nickel: Some Words With Himself . . . About the Wild West, the Pontiac, and the Last of the Seneca Chiefs," *Esquire*, March 1964.

19. Ibid.

20. Annette R. Cohen and Ray M. Druley, *The Buffalo Nickel* (Arlington, Va.: Potomac Enterprises, 1979), pp. 18-19.

21. In the *Coin World* reprint of the article from Home Insurance Co.'s Spring 1957 issue of *News From the Front* the author (likely Kenneth Dunshee) notes: "Recently, however, Mrs. Laura Gardin Fraser did recall to the present writer that the third Indian had been Big Tree, a Kiowa, who was a favorite model of Fraser on several occasions."

22. Norman C. Davis, *The Complete Book of United States Coin Collecting* (New York: Mcmillan Publishing, 1971; revised ed., New York: Mcmillan Publishing, 1976), p. 69.

23. Lee Martin, *Coin Columns* (Anaheim, Calif.: Clarke Printing, Anaheim, Calif., 1966), p. 59.

24. "Chief John Big Tree the Man on the Buffalo Nickel Highlights 1966 TNA Convention," *Numismatic News*, 25 April 1966, p. 16.

25. Dean Krakel, *End of the Trail: The Odyssey of a Statue* (Norman, Okla.: University of Oklahoma Press, 1973), p. 26.

26. Ibid.

27. Krakel links Fraser's comments to an interview. Ratzman, however, provides the same quote concerning Fraser's "objective," but ascribes its source to a letter of explanation from Fraser to the Mint. The quote concerning the Indian models could hail from the same unidentified source.

    The same quotes used by Krakel also appear in William Bridges, *Gathering of Animals: An Unconventional History of the New York Zoological Society* (New York: Harper and Row, 1974), p. 146, but without attribution. The New York Zoological Society, or Bronx Zoo, is often said to have been the site where Black Diamond, the bison named by Fraser as the model for the reverse of the Indian Head nickel, was held. Bridges was curator of publications for the society and did extensive research into the zoo's early history.

28. See John W. Dunn, "Silent Warwhoop Muffled Hooves," *Coins*, December 1973, pp. 64-65.
29. "The New Five Cent Piece," *The Numismatist*, March 1913, p. 130.

Chapter 2: A model bison

1. Dean Krakel, *End of the Trail: The Odyssey of a Statue* (Norman, Okla.: University of Oklahoma Press, 1973), p. 26. Krakel was director of the Cowboy Hall of Fame in Oklahoma City, Okla., and involved in a project to restore an original example of Fraser's *End of the Trail* statue. The quote is misattributed by Krakel to an article by syndicated writer Elmo Scott Watson, which appeared in the 4 March 1938 issue of the Shelby, Mich. *Oceana Herald*. The same quotes appears in William Bridges, *Gathering of Animals: An Unconventional History of the New York Zoological Society* (New York: Harper and Row, 1974), p. 146, but without attribution. Similar quotes are also found in 27 January 1913 *New York Herald* and in John W. Dunn, "Silent Warwhoop Muffled Hooves," *Coins*, December 1973, pp. 64-65. Dunn wrote:

   "There has been much speculation over why and how James Earle Fraser used the portrait of an Indian on the obverse and a buffalo or bison on the reverse of the proposed five-cent coin. As a boy in South Dakota, Fraser had seen buffalo. He actually used for his model Black Diamond, who had been born in the Central Park Zoo in 1893 and was a prime attraction. In 1912, Fraser lived in New York City not too far from the zoo and often sketched Black Diamond, because buffalo were considered very difficult to draw. Fraser often told the story that he desired to sketch Black Diamond in profile, but the shaggy animal always wanted to face the artist. Fraser had to pay the zoo attendant to attract Black Diamond's attention so that he could sketch the animal in profile."
2. Bridges, p. 146.
3. "Black Diamond is No More," *The Numismatist*, December 1915, p. 435.
4. Bridges, p. 71.
5. Ibid, p. 147.
6. Ibid.
7. Marianne F. Miller, in "A Sequel to the Buffalo Nickel," *Numismatic Scrapbook Magazine*, April 1957, tells a slightly different story. Quoting from an article by G.G. Goodwin, associate curator of the American Museum of Natural History, in a 1952 issue of *Nat-*

ural History Magazine, she reports that Charles R. Knight "was in the Zoological Museum in Washington when he spotted a man sketching a bull bison from a group that had been mounted at a request of W.T. Hornaday. Being an artist himself, he strolled over to see how the man was progressing. He found the man to be Mr. Baldwin, a Washington engraver, who was going to use the sketch for a buffalo note design. Mr. Knight offered to attempt the drawing, and much to his surprise, the offer was accepted. He decided, however, 'to use a living model instead of a stuffed one.' The article in the Natural History Magazine states, 'This incident probably gave rise to the erroneous report that the buffalo on the nickel was taken from a large bull killed by Hornaday in Montana and mounted for the National Museum.' This certainly gives a logical explanation for the mixed-up buffaloes."

8. Bridges, p. 148.
9. "The New Five-Cent Piece," *The Numismatist*, March 1913, p. 131.
10. Bridges, p. 149.
11. "Buffalo-Nickel Buffalo Deposed as Herd Leader," *The Numismatist*, August 1926, p. 441.

Chapter 3: An uncertain past

1. R.W. Julian, "Coin of Chance, Coin of Change, Coin of Conspiracy," *Coins*, May 1975, p. 69.
2. "Notes on the Convention," *The Numismatist*, October 1920, p. 466.
3. "The Rare 1913 Nickel," *The Numismatist*, January 1921, p. 17.
4. Julian, p. 70.
5. Ibid., p. 69.
6. "Deaths: Samuel W. Brown," *The Numismatist*, August 1944, p. 707. Brown was ANA member No. 808.
7. "Liberty 1913 Nickel Story Footnotes," *Numismatic Scrapbook Magazine*, April 1973, p. 372.
8. Arthur H. Lewis, *The Day They Shook the Plum Tree* (New York: Harcourt, Brace & World Inc., 1963), p. 247.
9. "Identifying 1913 Lib. Nickels," *Numismatic Scrapbook Magazine*, June 1961, p. 1709.
10. Abe Kosoff, *Abe Kosoff Remembers . . . 50 Years of Numismatic Reflections*, New York: Sanford J. Durst Numismatic Publications, 1981), p. 76.
11. Ibid, p. 75.
12. Interview with Tom Fruit, 1993. Same for later quotations.

13. J.V. McDermott, "The Fabulous $50,000 Nickel," *Coins*, September 1966, p. 53. McDermott adds that he couldn't bring himself to dismiss another of the story's theories — that a guard let go in 1918 for unknown reasons had found the dies and struck examples.
14. "Obituaries: J.V. McDermott A.N.A. LM 135," *The Numismatist*, December 1966, p. 1640.

Chapter 4: An unsinkable coin

1 Eric P. Newman and Kenneth E. Bressett, *The Fantastic 1804 Dollar* (Racine, Wis.: Whitman Publishing Co., 1962). The authors note that this story appeared in Ivan C. Michels, *The Current Gold and Silver Coins of All Nations*, Philadelphia, 1880, and in subsequent editions.
2. "With Editors and Advertisers," *The Numismatist*, November, 1899, p. 244.
3. "Will Remain Forever in Chicago," *The Numismatist*, February 1905, pp. 53-54.
4. "Counterfeits and Forgeries in Ancient and Modern Coins," *The Numismatist*, July 1937, p. 617.
5. "The 1804 Dollar Again," *The Numismatist*, March 1899, p. 56.
6. Ibid.

Chapter 5: An indecent coin

1. See Robert R. Van Ryzin, "An Artist's Written Word: The Letters of Hermon A. MacNeil Bring His Brilliant Career in Sculpture to Life," *Coins*, July 1988, pp. 66, 68-72.
2. J.H. Cline, *Standing Liberty Quarters*, (Dayton, Ohio: By the Author, 1976), p. 29.
3. Ibid.
4. Ibid., p. 32.
5. U.S. Department of Treasury, *Annual Report of the Director of the Mint for the Fiscal Year Ending June 30 1916 Including Report on the Production of the Precious Metals During the Calendar Year 1915* (Washington, D.C.: Government Printing Office, 1916), p. 8.
6. Cline, p. 45.
7. "New Designs Trouble Mint: Cannot Make Satisfactory Dies for Dimes, Quarters and Half Dollars," *Mehl's Numismatic Monthly*, October 1916, p. 130. The press notice (dated Sept. 15) from Philadelphia added that: "According to Dr. Albert A. Norris, chief clerk of the Philadelphia Mint, the die makers usually have trouble when designs are made by artists who are not familiar with

the mechanical problems." The December issue of Mehl's monthly recorded that new dimes were at hand, with some 3 million having been coined in October 1916 at Philadelphia.

8. Cline, p. 45.
9. Ibid., p. 46.
10. Don Taxay, *The United States Mint and Coinage: An Illustrated History From 1776 to the Present* (New York: Arco Publishing Co. Inc., 1966), p. 349.
11. Cline, p. 47.
12. Ibid., pp. 47-48.
13. "Designs of New Quarters Subject to Minor Change," *Mehl's Numismatic Monthly*, March 1917, p. 47.
14. U.S. Congress, House. *Congressional Record*, 65th Congress, 1st sess., 25 June 1917, p. 4223.
15. Cline, p. 50.
16. *The Lloyd M. Higgins, M.D. Collection and Other Properties*, Jan. 28-30, 1988 (Wolfeboro, N.H.: Auctions by Bowers and Merena, 1988), p. 41.
17. See "The New Half and Quarter Dollar," *The Numismatist*, January 1917, pp. 22-23.
18. "May Change Design of New Quarter Dollar," *The Numismatist*, March 1917, p. 111.
19. "New Dies for Quarter Dollar," *The Numismatist*, August 1917, p. 318.
20. "Revised Design for U.S. 1917 Quarter Dollars," *The Numismatist*, November 1917, p. 481.
21. "Editorial: Miss Liberty Now in a Gown of Mail?" *The Numismatist*, November 1917, pp. 470-471.

Chapter 6: Washington's silver

1. Sylvester S. Crosby, *The Early Coins of America* (Lawrence, Mass.: Quarterman Publications Inc., reprint ed., 1983), p. 364. First published by the author as *The Early Coins of America; and the Laws Governing Their Issue. Comprising Also Descriptions of the Washington Pieces of Unknown Origin, of the Seventeenth and Eighteenth Centuries, and the First Patterns of the United States Mint*, Boston, 1875.
2. Frank H. Stewart, *History of the First United States Mint and Its Operations*, (Frank H. Stewart Electric Co., 1924; reprint ed. as *History of the First United States Mint*, Lawrence, Mass: Quarterman Publications 1974), pp. 21. See also James Ross Snowden, *A Description of Ancient and Modern Coins in the the Cabinet of the*

United States. Snowden refers to the coin as a Washington half dime.

3. Ibid., pp. 21-22.
4. "After 99 Years," *The Numismatist*, May, 1943, p. 343.
5. Don Taxay, *The United States Mint and Coinage: An Illustrated History From 1776 to the Present* (New York: Arco Publishing Co. Inc., 1966), p. 72.
6. "More About the George Washington Half Disme," *The Numismatist*, July 1943, p. 527.
7. Andrew W. Pollock III, *United States Patterns and Related Issues* (Wolfeboro, N.H.: Bowers and Merena Galleries Inc., 1994), pp. 13-14.
8. Taxay, p. 71.
9. Walter Breen, "The United States Patterns of 1792," *The Coin Collector's Journal*, March-April 1954, pp 5-6. For his 1987 *Complete Encyclopedia* Breen quoted 1,500 as the number of specimens of the 1792 half disme minted.

Chapter 7: A pretend Indian?

1. "The Indian Head Cent," *The Numismatist*, November 1931, p. 804.
2. Reprinted in "Not Sara Longacre on Indian Cent," *Numismatic Scrapbook Magazine*, March 1951, p. 197.
3. Ibid.
4. Ibid.
5. Ibid., p. 198.
6. Ibid.
7. Walter Breen, "More About Longacre's Indian Cent Model," *Numismatic Scrapbook Magazine*, April 1951, p. 297.
8. Ibid, p. 298.
9. Walter Breen, "Our $3 Coin Born to Placate the Gold Interests," *Coins*, August 1968, p. 28.
10. Rev. Lindsay B. Longacre, "Longacre's Indian Cent Design," *Numismatic Scrapbook Magazine*, November 1951, p. 1006.
11. Joy Goforth, "Longacre's Goddess of Liberty," *Coin World* Jan. 4, 1984. According to Tom DeLorey, "Longacre: Unsung Engraver of the U.S. Mint," *The Numismatist*, October 1985, the *Coin World* article is reprinted from a November 1983 issue of *Mint Press*, a publication of the U.S. Mint, from which attribution is taken.
12. Rick Snow, *Flying Eagle and Indian Head Cents* (Seahurst, Wash.: Eagle Eye, 1994), p. 8.
13. Ibid.

Chapter 8: A perfect model

1. John H. Dryfhout, *The Work of Augustus Saint-Gaudens*, (Hanover, N.H.: University Press of New England, 1982), pp. 253-254.
2. Ibid., p. 35.
3. Homer Saint-Gaudens, "Roosevelt and Our Coin Designs: Letters Between Theodore Roosevelt and Augustus Saint-Gaudens," *Century Illustrated Monthly Magazine*, April 1920, p. 725. Ancients dealer Harlan Berk has a made a case for idea that although Roosevelt wanted an American Liberty striding forward, showing progress, what he got was a Victory goddess known as the *Nike of Paeonius* from the Temple of Zeus at Olympia in the Peloponnese. See, Harlan Berk, "Saint-Gaudens' Gold Piece Depicts Nike of Paeonius," *Numismatic News* 20 March 1990, p. 60. Others have claimed the inspiration was the *Winged Victory of Samothrace* shown on a Greek coin of Thrace.
4. Ibid.
5. Ibid.
6. Ibid.
7. Ibid., p. 726.
8. Ibid.
9. Weinman Papers, Archive of American Art, discovered by William E. Hagans.
10. Henry Hering, "History of the $10 and $20 Gold Coins of 1907 Issue," *The Numismatist*, August 1949, p. 455.
11. Ibid.
12. Ibid., p. 456.
13. Ibid.
14. Ibid.
15. "Want Native Face on Coin," *The Numismatist*, October-November 1907, p. 313.
16. William E. Hagans, "Author Contends Black Lady Modeled for Double Eagle," *Numismatic News*, 26 February 1991, p. 54.
17. Ibid.
18. Dryfhout, p. 219.
19. Burke Wilkinson makes a similar charge in *Uncommon Clay: The Life and Works of Augustus Saint-Gaudens* in relation to Homer Saint-Gaudens' attempt to obscure the memory of Augustus Saint-Gaudens' model and mistress, Davida Clark. Clark bore Saint-Gaudens' illegitimate son, Louis P. Clark.
20. Hagans, p. 54.
21. Ibid., p. 55.
22. Ibid.

23. Ibid.

24. Ibid.

25. Homer Saint-Gaudens, p. 733.

26. Adolph Weinman, Weinman Papers, Archive of American Art, discovered by William E. Hagans.

27. Hagans, p. 56.

28. Ibid., p. 55.

Chapter 9: Godless coins

1. "History of the Motto 'In God We Trust,' " U.S. Department of Treasury, *Twenty-Fourth Annual Report of the Director of the Mint to the Secretary of the Treasury for the Fiscal Year Ended June 30, 1896* (Washington, D.C.: Government Printing Office, 1897), p. 106.

2. Ibid. pp. 106-107.

3. Ibid., p. 107.

4. Homer Saint-Gaudens, "Roosevelt and Our Coin Designs: Letters Between Theodore Roosevelt and Augustus Saint-Gaudens," *The Century Illustrated Monthly Magazine* April 1920, p. 727.

5. Ibid.

6. Ibid.

7 Ibid, p. 728.

8. Letter from Theodore Roosevelt datelined Washington, Nov. 13, reprinted under "The Beginnings of Reform in Our Coinage," *The Numismatist*, January 1908.

Roosevelt's opinion was shared by others, including prominent numismatist H.O. Granberg, who complained:

"How puerile and irreverent sounds the motto of 'In God we trust' on money in these grasping, money-getting times. When prompted by the greed of gain and ofte[n] the most mercenary motives a call to 'mind your business' would be proper, while in this connection our present motto, 'In God we trust' is out of place, inappropriate and irreverent. Take it off!"

See H.O. Granberg, "The Fugio Cent of 1787, *Mehl's Numismatic Monthly*, November 1909, p. 169.

Chapter 10: A nation's dime

1. Don Taxay, *The U.S. Mint and Coinage: An Illustrated History From 1776 to the Present* (New York: Arco Publishing Co. Inc., 1966), p. 371.

2. Ibid., p. 375.

3. Cornelius Vermeule, *Numismatic Art in America: Aesthetics of the United States Coinage* (Cambridge, Mass: The Belknap Press of Harvard University Press, 1971), p. 208.
4. Ibid., pp. 208-209.
5. Interview with Dr. Selma Burke, 1993. Same for following quotations. See also, Robert R. Van Ryzin "Who Really Designed the Roosevelt Dime: Leading Black Sculptor Clings to Belief That Roosevelt Dime Design Hers, Not Sinnock's," *Numismatic News* 30 November 1993, p. 1.
6. " 'Peace' is Truman's Plea at Dedication of Roosevelt Plaque," Washington, D.C. *Evening Star*, Sept. 25, 1945.
7. "John R. Sinnock, Coin Designer," *Numismatic Scrapbook Magazine*, March 1946, p. 261.

Chapter 11: Initial controversy

1. Don Taxay, *The U.S. Mint and Coinage: An Illustrated History From 1776 to the Present* (New York: Arco Publishing Co. Inc., 1966), pp. 335, 337.
2.. Ibid., p. 337. A similar notation can be found in "1909 Cents Varieties: 'V.D.B.' Removed — Comments and Criticism, Impetus to Numismatics," *The Numismatist*, Sept.-Oct. 1909, p. 309.
3. "The Question Box: Some Questions Asked, the Answers to Which Will Interest the Young Collector," *Mehl's Numismatic Monthly*, December 1916, p. 157.
4. "Artist's Name on Coins Essential for History: A Letter From Victor D. Brenner," *The Numismatist*, Sept.-Oct. 1909, p. 276.
5. "The Artist and His Work," *Mehl's Numismatic Monthly*, September 1909, p. 147.
6. "1909 Cent Varieties: 'V.D.B.' Removed — Comments and Criticism, Impetus to Numismatics," *The Numismatist*. Sept.-Oct. 1909, p. 269.
7. Ibid.
8. Ibid.

Chapter 12: Ice cream money

1. U.S. Department of Treasury, *Annual Report of the Director of Mint to the Secretary of the Treasury for the Fiscal Year Ended June 30, 1894* (Washington, D.C.: Government Printing Office, 1894), p. 203.
2. "Editorial," *The Numismatist*, June 1900, p. 167. William A. Burd presented a thorough account of the known specimens of the 1894-S dime in his article in the February 1994 issue of *The Nu-*

mismatist, putting the number of traceable specimens at nine.

Citing research by Phil Carrigan, he discounts Mitchelson's discovery of an 1894-S dime. None apparently existed as part of Mitchelson's collection when it went to the Connecticut State Library in 1913.

See William A. Burd, "The Inscrutable 1894-S Dime: Continuing Research on This Highly Collectible Barber Issue Reveals Several Inconsistencies Regarding the Number and Pedigree of Extant Specimens," *The Numismatist*, February 1994, p. 287.

3. "Two Extreme Rarities in Recent U.S. Coinage, *The Numismatist*, April 1928, pp. 236-237.
4. James G. Johnson, "Is 1860-O Dime as Rare as Legendary 1894-S?" *Coin World*, June 27, 1973, pp. 50, 54.
5. "Two 1894-S Dimes Sold?" *Numismatic Scrapbook Magazine*, February 1951, p. 184.
6. Ira Goldberg, "Silence of the 1894-S Dime — Subtitle: What a Dealer Won't Do for a Big Deal," *Numismatic News*, 7 July 1992, p. 4.

Chapter 13: Twisted Tails

1. Walter Breen, *Walter Breen's Complete Encyclopedia of U.S. and Colonial Coins* (New York: F.C.I. Press, Doubleday, 1987), p. 311. Breen contends that Ross, a "hack writer from the Kansas City area," hoarded the dimes, which are rare only in mint state.
2. See Frank C. Ross, " 'Orphan Annie' (1844 Dime)," *Numismatic Scrapbook Magazine*, February 1946, p. 243.
3. See, for example, Bill The Coin Man, " 'Little Orphan Annie' 1844 Dimes," *The Numismatist*, October 1935, p. 699, and the first edition of *A Guide Book of United States Coins* (Racine, Wis.: Whitman Publishing Co., 1947).
4. "Stalin Initial Rumor Revived," *Numismatic Scrapbook Magazine*, March 1952, p. 298.
5. "He'll Find it There, All Right," *The Numismatist*, April 1926, p. 155.
6. "The Fasces on Our Dime," *The Numismatist*, October 1936, p. 823.
7. "The New Dime," *Mehl's Numismatic Monthly*, January 1917, p. 9.
8. "New Dimes May be Recalled: Coins Bear Initials of Designer, Held to be Violation of Law," *Mehl's Numismatic Monthly*, January 1917, p. 10.
9. Walter Breen, *Complete Encyclopedia*, p. 216.
10. "The Broken Sword on the New Peace Dollar," *The Numismatist*, February 1922, p. 101.

11. "The New Peace Coin Now in Circulation: Proposed by Mr. Zerbe and Fathered by the A.N.A., the Standard Silver Dollar Now Appears With New Designs," *The Numismatist*, February 1922, p. 63.
12. Ibid.
13. "No Change to be Made in Design of the Peace Dollar," *The Numismatist*, March 1922, p. 129.
14. Ibid.
15. "Criticizes the Eagle on Quarter Dollar," *The Numismatist*, March 1925, p. 179.
16. "The New Fifty-Cent Piece," *Mehl's Numismatic Monthly*, February 1917, p. 20.
17. Ibid.
18. "Newspaper Wants Coin Designs Changed," *Numismatic Scrapbook Magazine*, August 1942, p. 367.
19. Ibid., p. 368.
20. Ibid.
21. "Notes and Queries: Has a Lot of Trouble —" *The Numismatist*, May 1945, p. 450.
22. "Who Knows About Lincoln Cent With Two Heads?" *The Numismatist*, December 1931, p. 853.
23. Breen, p. 247.
24. Various sources. See, for example, Stuart James, "Case for the Gilded Nickel," *Money Talks: A Numismatic Anthology Selected From Calcoin News*, James L. Betton, ed., California State Numismatic Association, 1970.
25. "The 'Phoney' Fake or Racketeer Nickel," *Numismatic Scrapbook Magazine*, May 1960, p. 1557.
26. Lester V. Berrey and Melvin Van Den Bark, *The American Thesaurus of Slang*, 2nd ed., (New York: Thomas Y. Crowell Co., New York, 1953), p. 878.
27. "An Automobile for Four Mint Marks (?)," *Mehl's Numismatic Monthly*, January 1915, p. 194.
28. Ibid., p. 195.
29. "A Comment on 1922 'Plain' Cent," *Numismatic Scrapbook Magazine*, July 1964, p. 1860.
30. " 'Pennies From Heaven' in 1922," *The Numismatist*, July 1937, p. 645.
31. J.H. Cline, *Standing Liberty Quarters* (Dayton, Ohio: By the Author, 1976), pp. 55-59.

Bibliography

Books:

Berrey, Lester V. and Van Den Bark, Melvin. *The American Thesaurus of Slang.* 2nd ed. New York: Thomas Y. Crowell Co., 1953.

Betton, James L., ed. *Money Talks: A Numismatic Anthology Selected From Calcoin News.* California State Numismatic Association, 1970.

Bowers, Q. David. *The History of United States Coinage: As Illustrated by the Garrett Collection.* Los Angeles, Calif.: Bowers and Ruddy Galleries Inc., 1979.

Breen, Walter. *Walter Breen's Complete Encyclopedia of U.S. and Colonial Coins.* New York: F.C.I. Press, Doubleday, 1987.

Bridges, William. *Gathering of Animals: An Unconventional History of the New York Zoological Society.* New York: Harper and Row, 1974.

Cline, J.H. *Standing Liberty Quarters.* Dayton, Ohio: By the author, 1976.

Cohen, Annette R. and Druley, Ray M. *The Buffalo Nickel.* Arlington, Va.: Potomac Enterprises, 1979.

Crosby, Sylvester S. *The Early Coins of America.* Lawrence, Mass.: Quarterman Publications, reprint ed., 1983. Originally published by the author as *The Early Coins of America and the Laws Governing Their Issue. Comprising Also Descriptions of the Washington Pieces, the Anglo-American Tokens, Many Pieces of Unknown Origin, of the Seventeenth and Eighteenth Centuries, and the First Patterns of the United States Mint."* Boston, 1875.

Davis, Norman C. *The Complete Book of United States Coin Collecting.* New York: Mcmillan, revised ed., 1976.

Dryfhout, John H. *The Work of Augustus Saint-Gaudens.* Hanover, N.H.: University Press of New England, 1982.

Evans, George G. *Illustrated History of the United States Mint With a Complete Description of American Coinage, From the Earliest Period to the Present Time. The Process of Melting, Refining, Assaying, and Coining Gold and Silver Fully Described: With Biographical Sketches of Thomas Jefferson, Alexander Hamilton, Robert Morris, Benjamin Rush, John Jay Knox, James P. Kimball, Daniel M. Fox, and the Mint Officers From Its Foundation to the Present Time. To Which Are Added* a *Glossary of Mint Terms and the Latest Official Tables of the Annual Products of Gold and Silver in the Different States, and Foreign Countries, with Monetary Statistics of all Nations*. Philadelphia: George G. Evans, Publisher, new revised ed., 1888.

Julian, R.W. *Medals of the United States Mint: The First Century 1792-1892*. El Cajon, Calif.: Token and Medal Society, 1977.

Kosoff, Abe. *Abe Kosoff Remembers . . .50 Years of Numismatic Reflections*. New York: Sanford J. Durst Numismatic Publications, 1981.

Krakel, Dean. *End of the Trail: The Odyssey of a Statue*. Norman, Okla.: University of Oklahoma Press, 1973.

Lewis, Arthur H. *The Day They Shook the Plum Tree*. New York: Harcourt, Brace & World Inc., 1963.

Martin, Lee. *Coin Columns*. Anaheim, Calif.: Clarke Printing, 1966.

Newman, Eric P. and Bressett, Kenneth E. *The Fantastic 1804 Dollar*. Racine, Wis.: Whitman Publishing Co. 1962.

Pollock III, Andrew W. *United States Patterns and Related Issues*. Wolfeboro, N.H.: Bowers and Merena Galleries Inc., 1994.

Snow, Rick. *Flying Eagle and Indian Head Cents*. Seahurst, Wash.: Eagle Eye, 1994, p. 8.

Stewart, Frank H. *History of the First United States Mint and Its Operations*. Frank H. Stewart Electric Co., 1924; reprint ed. as *History of the First United States Mint*. Lawrence, Mass.: Quarterman Publications Inc., 1974.

Taxay, Don. *The U.S. Mint and Coinage: An Illustrated History From 1776 to the Present*. New York: Arco Publishing Co. Inc., 1966.

Tharp, Louise Hall. *Saint-Gaudens and the Gilded Era*. Boston: Little, Brown and Co., 1969.

Vermeule, Cornelius. *Numismatic Art in America: Aesthetics of the United States Coinage*. Cambridge, Mass.: The Belknap Press of Harvard University Press, 1971.

Yeoman, R.S. *A Guide Book of United States Coins*, Racine Wis.: Whitman Publishing, 1947

Journals and magazines:

"A Comment on 1922 'Plain' Cent." *Numismatic Scrapbook Magazine*, July 1964. p. 1860.

"After 99 Years." *The Numismatist*, May 1943, p. 343.

"An Automobile for Four Mint Marks(?)." *Mehl's Numismatic Monthly*, January 1915, pp. 194-195.

"Artist's Name on Coins Essential for History: A Letter From Victor D. Brenner." *The Numismatist*, Sept.-Oct. 1909, p. 276.

Bill The Coin Man. " 'Little Orphan Annie' 1844 Dimes." *The Numis-*

matist, October 1935, p. 699.

"Black Diamond is No More." *The Numismatist*, December 1915, p. 435.

Boston, William C. "Story of Our National Motto." *The Numismatist*, September 1962, pp. 1156-1159.

Breen, Walter. "The United States Patterns of 1792." *The Coin Collector's Journal*, March-April 1954, pp 5-6.

Breen, Walter. "More About Longacre's Indian Cent Model." *Numismatic Scrapbook Magazine*, April 1951, pp. 297-299.

Breen, Walter. "Our $3 Coin Born to Placate the Gold Interests." *Coins*, August 1968, pp. 27-31.

Brimelow, William. "The Indian Head Cent." *The Numismatist*, March 1937, p. 54.

"Buffalo-Nickel Buffalo Deposed as Herd Leader." *The Numismatist*, August 1926, p. 441.

Burd, William A. "The Inscrutable 1894-S Dime: Continuing Research on This Highly Collectable Barber Issue Reveals Several Inconsistencies Regarding the Number and Pedigree of Extant Specimens." *The Numismatist*, February 1994, pp. 228-289.

"Counterfeits and Forgeries in Ancient and Modern Coins." *The Numismatist*, July 1937, pp. 616-617.

"Criticizes the Eagle on Quarter Dollar." *The Numismatist*, March 1925, p. 179.

"Deaths: Samuel W. Brown." *The Numismatist*, August 1944, p. 707.

DeLorey, Tom. "Longacre: Unsung Engraver of the U.S. Mint." *The Numismatist*, October 1985, pp. 1970-1978.

De Shon, W.H. "The New Five-Cent Piece." *The Numismatist*, May 1913, p. 239.

"Designs of New Quarters Subject to Minor Change." *Mehl's Numismatic Monthly*, March 1917, p. 47.

Dunn, John W. "Silent Warwhoop Muffled Hooves." *Coins*, December 1973, pp. 64-65.

"Editorial." *The Numismatist*, June 1900, p. 167.

"Editorial: Miss Liberty Now in a Gown of Mail?" *The Numismatist*. November 1917, pp. 470-471.

Glaser, Alice. "The Indian-Head Nickel: Some Words With Himself . . . About the Wild West, the Pontiac, and the Last of the Seneca Chiefs," *Esquire*, March 1946.

Granberg, H.O. "The Fugio Cent of 1787, *Mehl's Numismatic Monthly*, November 1909, p. 169.

Hammer, Ted R. "Types of U.S. Nickel Coins." *Numismatic Scrapbook Magazine*, December 1943, pp. 721-729.

"He'll Find it There, All Right." *The Numismatist*, April 1926, p. 155.

Hering, Henry. "History of the $10 and $20 Gold Coins of 1907 Issue." *The Numismatist*, August 1949, p. 455.

"Identifying 1913 Lib. Nickels." *Numismatic Scrapbook Magazine*, June 1961, p. 1709.

"John R. Sinnock, Coin Designer." *Numismatic Scrapbook Magazine*, March 1946, p. 260-261.

Johnson, Don. "Two Guns White Calf — A Model Indian?" *Antique Week*, Feb. 27, 1989, pp. 1, 44.

Julian, R.W. "Coin of Chance, Coin of Change, Coin of Conspiracy." *Coins*, May 1975, pp. 64-70.

"Liberty 1913 Nickel Story Footnotes." *Numismatic Scrapbook Magazine*, April 1973, p. 372.

Longacre, Rev. Lindsay B. "Longacre's Indian Cent Design." *Numismatic Scrapbook Magazine*, November 1951, pp. 1006-1007.

"May Change Design of New Quarter Dollar" *The Numismatist*, March 1917, p. 111.

McDermott, J.V. "The Fabulous $50,000 Nickel," *Coins*, September 1966, pp. 52-53.

Miller, Marianne F. "A Sequel to the Buffalo Nickel." *Numismatic Scrapbook Magazine*. April 1957, pp. 657-659.

Miller, Marianne F. "Buffaloed by the Buffalo Nickel." *Numismatic Scrapbook Magazine*. October 1956, pp. 1697-1703.

"More About the George Washington Half Disme." *The Numismatist*, July 1943, p. 527.

Mosher, Stuart. "March of Dimes." *The Numismatist*, June 1955, pp. 620-621.

"New Designs Trouble Mint: Cannot Make Satisfactory Dies for Dimes, Quarters and Half Dollars." *Mehl's Numismatic Monthly*, October 1916, p. 130.

"New Dies for Quarter Dollar," *The Numismatist*, August 1917, p. 318.

"New Dimes May Be Recalled: Coins Bear Initials of Designer, Held to be Violation of Law." *Mehl's Numismatic Monthly*, January 1917, p. 10.

"Newspaper Wants Coin Designs Changed." *The Numismatic Scrapbook Magazine*, August 1942, pp. 367-368.

"Nickel Hoarding Continues." *Numismatic Scrapbook Magazine*, July 1939, p. 352.

"Nickels With Reeded Edges." *The Numismatist*, November 1941, p. 871.

"1909 Cent Varieties: 'V.D.B.' Removed — Comments and Criticism, Impetus to Numismatics." *The Numismatist*, Sept.-Oct. 1909, p. 269.

"No Change to be Made in Design of the Peace Dollar." *The Numismatist*, March 1922, p. 129.

"Notes and Queries: Has a Lot of Trouble —" *The Numismatist*, May 1945, p. 450.

"Notes on the Convention." *The Numismatist*. October 1920, p. 466.

"Not Sara Longacre on Indian Cent." *Numismatic Scrapbook Magazine*, March 1951, p. 197.

"Obituaries: J.V. McDermott A.N.A. LM 135." *The Numismatist*, December 1966, pp. 1639-1640.

" 'Pennies From Heaven' in 1922." *The Numismatist*, July 1937, p. 645.

Ratzman, Leonard J. "The Buffalo Nickel, A 50-Year-Old Mystery." *Whitman Numismatic Journal*, May 1964, pp. 21-29, and June 1964, pp. 27-32.

"Revised Design for U.S. 1917 Quarter Dollars." *The Numismatist*, November 1917, p. 481.

Roosevelt, Theodore. "The Beginnings of Reform in Our Coinage." *The Numismatist*, January 1908., pp. 6-7.

Ross, Frank C. " 'Orphan Annie' (1844 Dime)," *Numismatic Scrapbook Magazine*, February 1946, p. 243.

Saint-Gaudens, Homer. "Roosevelt and Our Coin Designs: Letters Between Theodore Roosevelt and Augustus Saint-Gaudens." *The Century Illustrated Monthly Magazine*, April 1920, pp. 721-736.

"Stalin Initial Rumor Revived." *Numismatic Scrapbook Magazine*, March 1952, p. 298.

"The Artist and His Work." *Mehl's Numismatic Monthly*, September 1909, p. 147.

"The Broken Sword on the New Peace Dollar." *The Numismatist*, February 1922, p. 101.

"The 1804 Dollar Again." *The Numismatist*, March 1899, pp. 53-56.

"The Fasces on Our Dime." *The Numismatist*, October 1936, p. 823.

"The Head on the Current Nickel." *The Numismatist*, July 1931, p. 485.

"The Indian Head Cent." *The Numismatist*, November 1931, p. 804.

"The New Dime." *Mehl's Numismatic Monthly*, January 1917, p. 9.

"The New Fifty-Cent Piece." *Mehl's Numismatic Monthly*, February 1917, p. 20.

"The New Five-Cent Piece." *The Numismatist*, March 1913, pp. 130-131.

"The New Half and Quarter Dollar." *The Numismatist*, January 1917, pp. 22-23.

"The New Peace Coin Now in Circulation: Proposed by Mr. Zerbe and Fathered by the A.N.A., The Standard Silver Dollar Now Appears With New Designs." *The Numismatist*, February 1922, pp. 57-66.

"The 'Phoney' Fake or Racketeer Nickel." *The Numismatic Scrapbook Magazine*, May 1960, p. 1557.

"The Question Box: Some Questions Asked, the Answers to Which Will Interest the Young Collector." *Mehl's Numismatic Monthly*, December 1916, p. 157.

"The Rare 1913 Nickel." *The Numismatist*, January 1921, p. 17.

Thompson, Walter. "The Half Disme of 1792." *Numismatic Scrapbook Magazine*, February 1960, pp. 299-305.

"Two 1894-S Dimes Sold?" *Numismatic Scrapbook Magazine*, February 1951, p. 184.

"Two Extreme Rarities in Recent U.S. Coinage. *The Numismatist*, April 1928, pp. 236-237.

"U.S. Coin Model Married." *The Numismatist*, August 1930, p. 519.

Van Ryzin, Robert R. "An Artist's Written Word: The Letters of Hermon A. MacNeil Bring His Brilliant Career in Sculpture to Life." *Coins*, July 1988, pp. 66, 68-71.

"Want Native Face on Coin." *The Numismatist*, October-November 1907, p. 313.

"Who Knows About Lincoln Cent With Two Heads?" *The Numismatist*, December 1931, p. 853.

"Will Remain Forever in Chicago." *The Numismatist*, February 1905, pp. 52-55.

"With Editors and Advertisers." *The Numismatist*, November, 1899, p. 244.

"With the Editor," *Mehl's Numismatic Monthly*, August-September 1916, pp. 101-104.

Newspapers:

"Chief John Big Tree the Man on the Buffalo Nickel Highlights 1966 TNA Convention." *Numismatic News*, 25 April 1966, p. 16.

Goforth, Joy. "Longacre's Goddess of Liberty." *Coin World*, 4 January 1984, pp. 1, 13, 18, 26, 30. Reprinted from November 1983 issue of *Mint Press*, a publication of the U.S. Mint.

Goldberg, Ira. "Silence of the 1894-S Dime — Subtitle: What a Dealer Won't Do for a Big Deal," *Numismatic News*, 7 July 1992, p. 4, 16, 17.

Hagans, William E. "Author Contends Black Lady Modeled for Double Eagle." *Numismatic News*, 26 February 1991, pp. 54-56.

Johnson, James G. "Is 1860-O Dime as Rare as Legendary 1894-S?" *Coin World*, 27 June 1973, pp. 50, 54.

" 'Peace' is Truman's Plea at Dedication of Roosevelt Plaque." Washington, D.C. *Evening Star* 25 September 1945.

" 'The Most Famous Coin' Famous Buffalo Nickel Only One of James E. Fraser's Great Works." *Coin World*, 23 December 1964, pp. 48, 54, 70. Reprint of article from Spring 1957 issue of *News from the Front*, a publication of the Home Insurance Co, New York, N.Y., edited by Kenneth Dunshee.

Van Ryzin, Robert R. "Which Indian Really Modeled." *Numismatic News*, 6 February 1990, pp.1, 64-67, 70.

Van Ryzin, Robert R. "Who Really Designed the Roosevelt Dime: Leading Black Sculptor Clings to Belief That Roosevelt Dime Design Hers, Not Sinnock's." *Numismatic News* 30 November 1993, pp. 1, 27-28, 34, 37-40.

Government documents:

U.S. Congress, House. *Congressional Record*, 65th Congress, 1st sess., June 25, 1917, p. 4223.

U.S. Department of Treasury. *Annual Report of the Director of the Mint for the Fiscal Year Ended June 30, 1916 and also Report on the Production of Precious Metals in the Calendar Year 1915*. Washington, D.C.: Government Printing Office, 1916.

U.S. Department of Treasury. *Twenty-Fourth Annual Report of the Director of the Mint to the Secretary of the Treasury for the Fiscal Year Ended June 30, 1896*. Washington, D.C.: Government Printing Office, 1897.

U.S. Department of Treasury. *Twenty-Second Annual Report of the Director of Mint to the Secretary of the Treasury for the Fiscal Year Ended June 30, 1894*. Washington, D.C.: Government Printing Office, 1894.

Auction catalogs:

The Lloyd M. Higgins, M.D. Collection and Other Properties, Jan. 28-30, 1988. Wolfeboro, N.H.: Auctions by Bowers and Merena, 1988.